Advance Praise

Bose completely changed the way I think about networking, and I'm excited to try her joy-centered approach. *The Stay Joyful Method* pushes you to get clear, not just on your goals, but also on what excites you, which we often forget to consider. Instead of the usual surface-level check-ins, she invites you to name your joy and build from there. That clarity turns networking into something energizing and aligned with the kind of community where you can truly thrive.

—**Heather Meloy**
Director, Sustainability and Social Impact, PwC

The Stay Joyful Method reframes joy as the ultimate strategic advantage. Bose Akadiri reminds us that joy is not incidental to success. It fuels it. As a purpose-driven leader, she offers both inspiration and practical wisdom for anyone seeking impact without losing themselves in the process.

—**Alicia Wilson, Esq.**
Vice President for Civic Engagement and Opportunity, Johns Hopkins University

I absolutely love how Bose reframed joy as a must-have rather than a nice-to-have. She's truly building the business case for joy and empowering us all to incorporate the use of joy in every aspect of our lives. As a team leader, I now better recognize the importance of prioritizing my own joy, so it brings joy into the team as well.

—Jim Roth
Founder and President, A New Energy
Dean Emeritus, Oklahoma City University School of Law
Director, Phillips Murrah Law Firm

Joy is often perceived as a reward for success. Bose flips that idea, showing how joy can be the starting point for living and working with greater intention, purpose, productivity, and impact.

—Stacy Sharpe
Executive Vice President
Chief Communications Officer, Verizon

Using joy as your offense and defense is a genius concept. This book is a timely reflection on how to capture and maintain your joy. Bose has provided the tools to help us better understand ourselves and live life on our terms, through the lens of inner joy rather than external validation. This book can support multiple generations, as joy is a lifelong goal, and Bose's book is an excellent resource to ensure that joy is in your DNA.

—Kenneth Jones
Chief Operating Officer and Chief Equity Officer,
John D. and Catherine T. MacArthur Foundation

I've been leading teams for over twenty years and *The Stay Joyful Method* is what we need right now. Through times of turbulence, Bose frames joy as a tool to be used for clarity, confidence, and planning.

—Ebony Beckwith
Founder, Framework

Bose is one of those rare people who lifts everyone around her. From the moment I met her when she first moved to Chicago, she has always had that same joyful spirit. Her message about joy is powerful and deeply needed right now, and I'm so excited she's sharing it in this book.

—Jonny Imerman
Co-Founder, CLOZTALK
Co-Founder, Imerman Angels

The Stay Joyful Method centers leading with joy as an effective life strategy and provides a helpful framework for cultivating joy. It reminds us that joy is personal, but flourishes in community.

—Tiana Conley
Vice President Corporate Brand and Purpose

I didn't know how much I needed *The Stay Joyful Method* until I picked up my personal copy. From the "recognizing your joy" step in the Vision and Goals Method™ to realizing that "joy connects you," I believe I have the tools to redefine my personal and professional success. I'm ready to reclaim my joy, and I'm thrilled I have a method to make it happen!

—Dr. Veronica Appleton, PhD
Corporate Executive, Children's Author, and Scholar

The Stay Joyful Method is truly an inspiring book. Bose doesn't just stop at using joy in good times; she also addresses the difficulty of finding and claiming joy in the midst of grief and challenging decisions. We all face difficult times in our lives, and how we face those difficulties has a profound impact on our lives.

Bose was a young woman when she found her way to our church, and she brought her beautiful spirit and smile with her. She first became a valuable member and volunteer, then later joined our staff as part of our hospitality team. Her faith and joy were at the forefront of her life.

—Dr. Bob and Marsha Long
St. Luke's Methodist Church

Bose outlines practical steps and a method for how we make joy the guiding light and driving force of our purpose and our work. Leading global teams today is fraught with challenges, and Bose's insights help me increase trust and optimism to power teams forward.

—Dave Holloman
Senior Partner

What I appreciate most about *The Stay Joyful Method* is how Bose reframes joy from a fleeting feeling into a practice. Through stories, research, and reflection, she shows how joy can guide our decisions, strengthen our relationships, and help us lead with greater clarity and intention. It's an invitation to build a life and leadership style rooted in what truly matters.

—Daniel Horgan
CEO, CoLabL

THE
STAY
JOYFUL
METHOD

THE STAY JOYFUL METHOD

USING JOY AS A TOOL TO RISE, LEAD, AND REDEFINE SUCCESS

Bose Akadiri

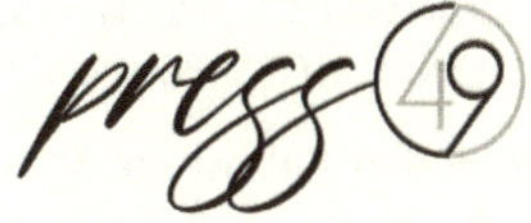

Press 49
4980 South Alma School Road
Suite 2-493
Chandler, Arizona 85248

Published by Press 49, a division of BMH Companies, Chandler, Arizona.

Volume pricing is available for bulk orders from corporations, associations, and others. For bulk order details and media inquiries, please contact Press 49 at info@press49.com or 833.PRESS49 (833.773.7749).

FIRST EDITION

Library of Congress Control Number: 2026905836

ISBN (hardback): 978-1-953315-66-3
ISBN (paperback): 978-1-953315-67-0
ISBN (eBook): 978-1-953315-68-7

SEL031000 SELF-HELP / Personal Growth / General
SEL016000 SELF-HELP / Personal Growth / Happiness
BUS046000 BUSINESS & ECONOMICS / Motivational
BUS107000 BUSINESS & ECONOMICS / Personal Success

Interior and cover design by Medlar Publishing Solutions Pvt Ltd., India

Printed in the United States of America

Table of Contents

PART III: JOY THAT SUSTAINS YOU

PART IV: JOY THAT ENDURES

Foreword

When Bose and I were first introduced through a mutual friend, our conversation began with something deceptively simple: a coat.

Years ago, at nineteen, I purchased a coat that could double as a maternity coat. I knew I wanted to start a family soon after college, and I believed in preparing early for the life I intended to build. Bose told me that story resonated deeply with her because her mother bought her a suit from The Limited every sale season during college so she would be fully prepared for her first job after graduation.

Two young women. Two different paths. The same principle.

Live on your own terms. But prepare for them.

Intentionality has shaped every major decision in my life and career. Ambition without preparation is simply desire. Ambition with a plan becomes power. In my experience, the people who achieve meaningful success do not drift into it. They decide. They prepare. They execute. They adjust.

In speaking with Bose, I recognized that same discipline beneath her warmth. When she shared her story of leaving Oklahoma City and moving to Chicago without a job secured, I immediately connected with the calculated nature of that risk. I have taken risks throughout my career, including stepping into roles where the odds were not necessarily in my favor, but those risks were never reckless. They were informed. They were intentional. They were aligned with the life I wanted to build.

This book is not about ignoring obstacles or pretending risks and challenges do not exist. It is about making intentional choices in the face of them. It is about defining success for yourself and refusing to outsource that definition to external expectations. It is about building a plan that integrates your ambitions with your values while experiencing joy.

The Stay Joyful Method challenges a deeply ingrained belief in our culture: that joy comes after achievement. Bose makes a compelling case that joy is not the reward at the end of the journey but the strategic advantage that fuels it. As leaders and professionals, we often postpone joy in pursuit of goals, believing that discipline must replace delight. Bose reframes that narrative. She argues, persuasively and practically, that joy strengthens resilience, sharpens clarity, and improves performance.

Readers will learn how to translate vision into actionable goals, how to build authentic professional networks, and how to lead teams in a way that produces results for individuals and organizations alike. Bose blends research, lived experience, and practical tools to show that joy, when treated as a strategic resource, can drive sustainable success.

If you are feeling externally accomplished yet internally unfulfilled, this book will challenge you to reassess your foundation. If you are ambitious but unsure how to align your drive with deeper meaning, this framework will provide direction. And if you are ready to lead and live more intentionally, Bose offers both encouragement and structure.

I'm a big believer in creating success on your own terms which requires clarity, courage, and discipline. Bose adds one more powerful element to that formula: joy. In doing so, she invites you not only to achieve more, but to build a life that feels fully yours.

That is a risk worth taking.

—Shellye Archambeau
Author of *Unapologetically Ambitious: Take Risks,
Break Barriers, and Create Success on Your Own Terms*

How to Stay Joyful: A Practical Method of How to Live, Work, and Lead

JOURNEYS IN JOY: SHE RELEASED FEAR TO BLOSSOM INTO HER CHOSEN CAREER

I read Cherrell's email in astonishment. She shared that after declaring her dream job for the first time to a room of strangers at the Vision and Goals Party, she had made the career pivot. Candidly, I knew the methodologies I'd created worked for me and a few others, but I wasn't sure that they worked for the masses. This was the moment I learned that it did.

Let me share Cherrell's story with you. She hated her job. Hated it! Does this sound familiar? She followed the rules, yet she told me, "I was unhappy in my career and also not doing well financially."

Reflecting on her state of being before the Vision and Goals Party, she knew what she wanted to do but lacked a plan to get there.

"When it has come to goals, my mindset was usually on the big picture and not the smaller steps to reach the goal," meaning she had the big, dream-sized vision and just needed a pathway to get there.

Hearing her share, "I usually would just rely on motivation when it'd come to goals" and "One bad day could derail me. Relying solely on motivation worked only temporarily," I knew she needed milestone goals to check off a list and celebrate over time rather than waiting to celebrate at the finish line.

Cherrell's energy was depleted to the point of debilitation. I was curious what she had tried in the past.

She let me know, "I would try to practice DJing during my free time, but I'd be so wiped out from work that all I wanted to do was just lie on the couch, rest, and dissociate."

Her role was sucking the life out of her. She was running on fumes, and going at it solo was draining, as it would be to anyone.

That day at the Vision and Goals party, the entire room witnessed Cherrell come alive when she shared her desire to be a DJ.

Later, she would tell me, "My biggest 'aha' moment was that my life wasn't aligned with my Joy Bubble. My idea of a life well lived didn't reflect my life at that time. My job at that time was definitely draining the joy out of me, and while I wasn't able to leave it at that time, I knew I really had to fight for my joy."

I now know that spark in her eye was because that's the moment she made a conscious choice to reclaim her joy.

I had to know exactly what sparked that aha moment for her!

Cherrell let me know, "The Joy Bubble and the part where I envisioned myself in ten years. Reflecting on what brings me joy and who I truly want to be in the future energized me. It made me excited to start taking steps towards my desires."

That was it. Joy was the spark that ignited her quest.

When I read her email about her first paid DJ gig, I sensed a tone of "This is all I've done so far," so I couldn't help but respond with a list of all the small steps that got her to that big accomplishment.

Getting a paid DJ gig meant she had researched DJ schools, rearranged her schedule to attend courses, adjusted her budget to afford schooling, built connections during class, and, above all, completed DJ schooling. After all of that, she still had to market herself well enough to get paid for the work. I was counting at least five micro accomplishments, whereas she was only counting one macro accomplishment. Once I sent that response, she was elated to share how she celebrated her big wins!

Now I realize Cherrell sacrificed even more as she later shared, "I quit my second job in order to take DJ classes at Miyagi Records. My joy and goals mattered more than the extra money, even though I needed it."

She literally put her livelihood on the line to amplify her joy. Cherrell is brave, and she had the clarity needed to take strategic risks.

When it came to landing paid gigs, Cherrell said, "For my graduation, I performed a thirty-minute set in front of my cohort, staff, and guests. It was recorded live. Having that recording helped kick off my DJ career because it was tangible proof of my talent."

Being in a role that depletes you can spill over into other areas of your life. As Cherrell said, after transitioning careers, "My stress levels are definitely down, and life is more stimulating and interesting. Even my social life has thrived."

It brings me joy to share that her transformation is one of many journeys in joy you'll read in this book. The Stay Joyful Method and its sub-methodologies have been shifting mindsets and changing the lives of people from all walks of life for years.

Cherrell is leveraging joy to build a life that she finds rewarding, whereas she could have easily followed the predestined pathway.

This is why she can proudly say, "Life feels a lot fuller now. I've never had a day job that felt fulfilling, so it's amazing to have fulfillment elsewhere. I really feel like I'm making something out of my life."

She's even returned to the marketing field with greater clarity, ready to be stimulated and build on her prior experience. This creates a sense of purpose for Cherrell both professionally and personally.

Her biggest mindset shift is, "I approach goal setting with a fear of staying the same. I deserve to see what's on the other side of pursuing my goals."

I had to pause when I read these words from her. She's shifted from the fear of not following the unwritten rules of life to the fear of not being true to herself.

Later in this book, we'll talk about the resulting community you build with clear goals. I can't help but see the parallels of what Cherrell shared as an unexpected impact of this work on her life: "I'm much more protective of my peace now in all aspects of my life. I'd say an unexpected benefit is the way my social life has thrived. I have so many friends and connections now that I didn't have just a couple of years ago."

She focused on herself and became a magnet for the kind of network that was fertile ground for her growth.

Cherrell's closing sentiments enlightened me as she said, "I'd want them to know that they deserve to see what's on the other side of pursuing their goals. Their joy matters, and it's worth fighting for. Life is to be enjoyed."

Hearing her put it that way truly showcases that claiming your joy positions you for success.

The unique part about the methodologies that you'll learn in this book is that they are ongoing rather than a point in time.

Cherrell commented, "I'm also very proud of how I've continued to invest in myself," which I'm also proud of her for. Once you begin to let joy lead as your decision-making compass, you are empowered to grow deeper in all areas of life in perpetuity.

Joy is the Foundation of Goal Setting, Not Just the Reward

Most people are taught to treat joy as a reward to be longed for. That approach works until it doesn't. You chase joy until an unknown point in time, and once you arrive at the finish line, it always seems to move. Your accomplishments get whisked by as though it's just another Tuesday afternoon, nothing special, and no recognition.

Joy predicts life satisfaction through resilience, not just "feeling good." Research shows that people didn't become more satisfied just because they felt happier. "Joy involves physical and cognitive freedom to 'broaden and build,' which involves exploring and creating new...schemas and...resources."[1]

In this book, joy functions more like your foundation. It's your starting point, not your finish line. Your joy is unique to you, but it's also a practical tool that guides your decision-making. This book is about being rooted in joy from the beginning.

Life is busy, so it's easy to get caught up in your day-to-day to-do list without considering your future self. Throughout this book, we're going to reverse the process by starting in the future, then building actions that will make her proud.

Ensure your short-term goals align with your long-term vision by naming your long-term goals, then building your to-do list with actions that support them. This is how you transition into creating a strategy for your life that you can follow rather than a reactionary string of disconnected to-do lists. You're working hard, so why not work hard toward your dream life?

My First Ten-Year Vision

My current ten-year vision is so big it scares me, but so did the last one. I took baby steps to get there and remained faithful that it could happen, while I ignored the doubts and doubters.

My initial vision was that I wanted to live in a more diverse city, I wanted an international airport, I wanted public transportation, I wanted to work at a Fortune 500, I wanted to own my own business, I wanted to travel the world with friends, I wanted financial stability, and I wanted to build a family.

And that's it. The vision led me to research and learn what could make that vision, driven by joy, possible.

When I first developed my life strategy, I didn't know the name of my company or the city I'd live in. Those weren't the things I needed to know to make the decision. What I needed for myself was a vision. Something I believed in and could build toward over time.

This is what I wrote down in February of 2014 for my life at the age of twenty-nine:

> *I live an exciting life full of love and growth in a city I adore! I am continually learning about my own body while joyfully sharing my knowledge of health and nutrition with others. I regularly schedule excursions around the world with my husband, kiddos, and best girls (Lauren, Fallon, and mom).*

I am the founder of Royal Barkery, a successful organic dog treat company that improves the life of man's best friend through nutritious treats & philanthropy. My darling puppy love, Chanel, has aged gracefully yet still enjoys play dates and traveling with me. Chanel is a registered therapy dog with monthly visits bringing licks and love to hundreds of people each year.

I sit on boards with organizations that improve the quality of life for disadvantaged women. I am honored to facilitate the means for them to have everything from interview attire to access to higher education and more. I have my CYT 200 and use it while teaching therapeutic yoga classes at my local women's shelter.

Some things changed along the way, but the essence remained the same.

You have to have grace with yourself and understand that your journey will most likely not be a linear path and that changes will arise. You are human after all, which means you are growing and learning more each day. This includes learning about yourself, which can lead to changes in your joy and, in turn, in the vision for your life.

It is important during this process to give yourself space to grow into it more deeply. I typically do a vision and goals session with myself at least once a year. It's a great way to refresh myself to ensure alignment with my joy, vision, and goals as I evolve.

A life without growth would be boring! That's why you must get comfortable with change as it is inevitable...within yourself as well as the world around you. I get that change can be scary and often uncomfortable, since you were used to the way things were and were familiar with how to keep things as they were. Change brings about several unknowns. Focus on the positive possibilities and outcomes of change rather than the negatives of losing what currently exists. We can honor and be grateful for our past selves, but not live as them in the present. For example, I love baby Bose. She was so naive in some ways and lived a different life than I do now. The difference is that she learned, grew, and evolved.

I actually prefer the word *evolve* to *change*. Evolving includes growth and gratitude for the person you once were. Evolving is much deeper than changing. Change feels like a light switch just going on and then off, but your journey will be deeper than that, deeper than simply flipping a switch, and you're there at the finish line.

One change can put a kink in things, BUT everything changing at once is a whole different story.

What I realized is what my bestie, Lauren, has always said, "You're the master of your destiny."

She says it so plainly and simply, and she has since we were in college. I used to hear her say it and brush by, sometimes even wondering how? But now I realize it's actually one of the most profound things that I go back to anytime I have a doubt or am feeling scared about something the world has brought my way. Being the master of my own destiny means that all the shifts are the result of my own decisions.

My decisions for peace have brought temporary chaos while I figure out my new norm, but there is always beauty in the process. Being the master of my own destiny means it is literally time for me to create my dream life, crafting it like a fine piece of art. And it's time for you to create your dream life, too! Let's chart it out so there's less confusion and more clarity.

You (and Your Team) Deserve Joy

When I use the word *joy* here, I'm not referencing generic happiness. I'm talking about your core decision-making rubric, which strategically aligns your life. The physical manifestation of this joy can feel like an inner longing for more of an experience. Your joy is unlike anyone else's. It's a passion you can't live without. Think about an inspiration that feels like the source of your existence. Joy is motivating.

Once at an event, I met someone new. The first thing I asked her was, "What brings you joy?"

She shared that she really likes problem-solving and enjoys a challenge. She went on and on, and her face lit up brighter and brighter as she shared what brought her joy. I loved it. I loved hearing about her joy, and I loved seeing it in her body language. She has joy, and she knows her joy.

We don't all know our joy. And that's okay. You're here now, and I'm going to challenge you to dig deep within and define your joy because I am one-hundred percent sure that your joy is better than any worldly expectation that's been previously placed upon you.

What is a Worldly Expectation?

It's the shoulds. When people say you should do this or you should do that, it's not that they don't wish you well. It's typically the opposite. It's that they only know one option, and it seems like a safe option that will ensure you have a good life, make money, or accomplish anything you're trying to. The shoulds are the linear options that are like coloring inside the lines, but you don't have to take that route. You can color outside the lines and be great, potentially even greater!

For some, the shoulds take the form of questions stemming from societal pressures. When you're younger, everyone is asking where you'll go to school, college, etc. Then you pick a school and aren't even enrolled yet, and people are asking what you'll major in. Then you pick a major, and people are asking where you'll get a job. Then you get a job, and people are asking when you'll get a promotion and who you're dating. Then you start dating, and people are asking when you're getting married. Then you're married, and people are asking when you'll have kids. Then you have a kid, and people are asking when you'll have the second one. Research has revealed that these societal pressures are, in fact, "barriers to joy."[2]

Well, guess what? You have options outside of those!!! You actually have a plethora of options, but no one talks about those or "shoulds on you" about those. This is why the other options are so easy to forget about.

One of my clients once told me that her whole life was pre-planned, and then one day she woke up and wondered how she got there and what was next. She said that's where I come in to help you design your life (and re-design it if needed).

It's hard to tap into our inner joy because the world is constantly presenting and pushing its shoulds upon us. It takes determination, grit, and perseverance to tap into our own joy. We have to be intentional about our joy to ignite it, be protective of it to sustain it, and be proud of it to spread it.

Joy takes work. It really does. It's not just something that comes (and stays) easily. I know I've lost mine before, but that's exactly what makes me treasure it even more.

The problem is that no one is talking about, asking about, or including joy in their plans. They're talking about distractions, or as I like to call them, "the shiny objects," which are the fluff that is presented to us as a quick fix.

I recall a time when I lost my joy due to a toxic professional collaboration. It was high-stakes, as there were time constraints and I'd poured a great deal of money into the project. The partner I selected wasn't performing, giving excuse after excuse. The other partners on the project got irritated. I was spiraling, trying to hold them accountable. This one faulty partner was disrupting the entire team. I began to doubt my decision to choose them as a partner. This is when fear crept in. I was losing my joy, and so was my team.

I finally replaced the partner with a more competent one. During the first full team meeting, all partners were visibly and audibly excited as the team was aligned. The new partner was collaborative rather than combative when asked clarifying questions. Not only was my joy restored, but the entire team's was as well.

In addition to talking about joy, it is helpful to recount the moments when joy is lost. As you move forward, there's an appreciation for understanding how joy was lost.

The norm is to set a goal, then celebrate once it's been achieved. But what if we got serious with ourselves about what brings us joy, then set goals that amplify that joy? Flip the script. Life is precious, and there's no reason to wait for some distant goal to celebrate.

High achievers don't avoid joy because they don't value it. It happens because of time constraints, pressure to perform, and/or perfectionism.

Postponing joy increases the risk of burnout because you go nonstop without pausing for anything, let alone recognition. This is mainly because we high-achieving women will keep moving the celebratory achievement goal post and never end up seeing joy.

That sounds awful! But it's how we live, myself included, before I realized the key to it all was starting with joy, letting joy guide your decision-making, existing in joy on your journey, and amplifying your joy every step of the way.

The thing is, goals are hard to accomplish; therefore, when there are tough times, and you want to give up, joy will sustain you because you know the long-term goal aligns with your specific/distinct joy factors.

Joy is your psychological safety weapon, which you can call upon at any time. Joy is at the heart of everything I teach in my keynote speeches and corporate training workshops.

The Stay Joyful Method is about threading joy throughout your life, from goal setting to building community to aligning teams, letting joy lead every step of the way. The concepts in this book build on each other; however, you can also use each chapter as a standalone lesson. They will support you in not only gaining a deeper understanding of your own joy but also in how to become a fierce defender of your joy.

Everything I teach, whether in leadership rooms, professional development settings, or one-on-one coaching, builds from this foundation. Joy informs how people clarify their vision, communicate their value, and lead in ways that create mutual benefit rather than burnout. This book brings those principles together in one place, not as separate skills, but as a single way of operating.

In this book, we're going to explore joy in ways you might not have previously. We start with this introduction to joy, then flow into the following:

PART I: Joy That Moves You

Chapter 1: Why Joy Is the Smartest Starting Point

Chapter 2: Plan From Joy, Not Pressure

PART II: Joy That Connects You

Chapter 3: Guard What Gives You Clarity

Chapter 4: Build Community Without Performing

Chapter 5: Choose the People Who Multiply Your Joy

PART III: Joy That Sustains You

Chapter 6: Create Alignment Across Your Whole Life

Chapter 7: Align Your Team With Purpose

Chapter 8: Lead in a Way People Want to Follow

PART IV: Joy That Endures

Chapter 9: When Fear Shows Up

Chapter 10: Holding Joy in Hard Seasons

Chapter 11: Make Joy a Way of Life

By the end of this book, you'll not only know how to choose joy for yourself but also how to incorporate practices within your lifestyle that sustain your joy. You will learn to be a model of joy for others, thereby building and sustaining joy in your community. You'll even discover tactics to incorporate joy within your leadership style, thus creating aligned, thriving teams.

I designed this book with you in mind—the busy, sometimes stressed-out, pressed-for-time human. The book is designed linearly; however, it's also designed so you can easily pick up any chapter and get support on that topic.

At all times, you can use joy as your offense to set the tone of how you live your life and/or your defense to protect and maintain your momentum of building the life you desire.

This book is more than teaching and learning. It's about action. Just like my keynotes and training workshops, I aim to empower you to take your next best steps.

JOY JUMPSTART

Each chapter closes with a Joy Jumpstart, a simple way to move joy from reflection into real life action. Here's what I've noticed, and you might recognize this, too. Having a prompt to support putting learnings into action can be helpful.

Joy Jumpstarts are not about adding more to your plate. Together, these moments help joy become something you practice daily, share intentionally, and advocate for boldly.

JOY THAT MOVES YOU

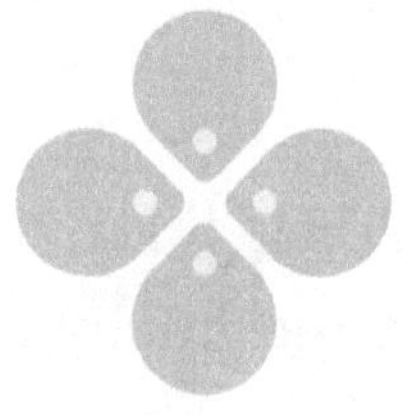

JOURNEYS IN JOY: FROM GOO TO BUTTERFLY THROUGH INTENTIONAL STRUCTURE

I watched Jill Miller walk away from a stable corporate career and jump into the unknown. She'd spent years selling industrial equipment—conveyors, grinders, optical sorters—building someone else's legacy. But she wanted her kids to be proud of the work she did. She wanted to matter.

So, she jumped.

"I was like the goo in the caterpillar," Jill describes those early months of entrepreneurship. "Not a caterpillar and not a butterfly. I was in this liminal, directionless space."

For a year, she was on the teacups ride at the carnival, spinning. She had vision. She had passion. But she had no plan.

"You do a lot of planning, but it's constantly changing," she reflects. "You just keep getting handed off and handed off, and you're spinning."

This is the trap of the ambitious without structure: knowing what you want to change but not knowing how to actually change it.

Then, in January 2024, Jill arrived at the Vision and Goals Party, exhausted and finally ready to ask herself the questions nobody had forced her to ask.

"One of the things we don't do enough in life is pause and ask ourselves what our values are," she realized. "Ask ourselves what is important."

The shift wasn't her ambition. It was her approach.

She learned what would become her operating principle: "Energy flows where intention goes."

And more practically, she learned the five-step Vision and Goals Method™. This was not abstract ideas but concrete categories requiring intentional planning and consistent execution.

"It's the execution where you get change," Jill explains. "It's kind of like pulling toilet paper off the roll, and it gets smaller. It's how I think of going to the gym: If you want to get smaller, one sheet at a time."

So, Jill did something radical: She applied the same continuous improvement philosophy she'd learned in twenty years of factory floor automation work to her own life.

When a machine goes down, they'll spend hundreds of thousands of dollars to understand why. But when a person isn't operating efficiently, we just shrug and say, "Yeah, they were a cost anyway."

Her realization: What if I treated myself like the asset I am?

She stopped trying to be perfect in all areas. She got clear on her values—people as assets, continuous improvement, legacy, and then structured her time around them intentionally.

"As long as my girls are happy, we are all going to be happy," she adds.

This wasn't surrender. It was alignment. It was knowing that trying to be 100 percent in everything meant being mediocre in everything.

But here's what nobody expects: The moment Jill stopped spinning and started structuring, everything accelerated. Her business, Lunum, grew from a 4:00 a.m. moment to over $1 million in annual revenue. She's in the middle of a seed round for fundraising. Lunum has positively changed how 40,000 people are viewed at work. They're tracking data on 19.5 million people, understanding what good looks like.

Outside of Lunum, she hosts *SpondyCast*, a podcast for people with chronic disease. They hit their one hundredth episode, an accomplishment she's "probably most proud of in life beyond [her] kids and beyond building Lunum."

She takes time at the ashram to reset and invest in herself so she can invest in others. She shows up for her daughters. She shows up for the work. When asked what changed her everyday life, Jill closed with the insight that matters most: "Consistency. Consistency in your approach is everything. You can't go to the bar three nights a week or sit on your phone scrolling six hours a day and expect you're going to achieve your goals. It's about consistency."

Her yoga teacher asked her a question that stuck: "Are you ready to do what it takes? And are you willing to do what it takes to get what you want?"

Jill's answer, lived out every day, is yes. Not through perfection. Not through intensity. Through structure. Through intention. Through knowing that when you plan from joy, name your values, structure your time, and commit to consistency, the going around in circles stops, and real movement begins.

Now you'll find Jill transforming how organizations view and develop their people. She's also a dedicated advocate for the Spondylitis Association of America™, a mother, and someone who understands that sustainable achievement happens through intentional structure, not heroic effort.

CHAPTER 1

Why Joy Is the Smartest Starting Point

Opinions are coming at you from left, right, above, below, and all around. You begin to ruminate on a decision, as there are as many options to choose from as there are menu items at The Cheesecake Factory. Your pro-con list has an equal number of pros and cons. How do you know you're making the right decision, the best decision? You seek clarity by asking peers for advice, googling until you're on the sixth page of search results, and getting wrapped up in the Reddit conversations on the topic. This overcomplication goes on for days, sometimes weeks, or even months, then you crash without making a clear decision. The complications and answer-seeking lead to sheer mental and physical exhaustion. You're depleted, yet you still don't have your answer.

Pause.

What if this cycle of endless rumination isn't about fear or your inability to come to a conclusion?

Perhaps it's about too many external inputs shaping your plan to progress. External expectations can drive you to a level of perfectionism that simply isn't realistic, amplifying anxiety around your choices. The pressure to constantly "get it right" combined with endless options overstimulates the mind.

The real problem isn't that people don't know what they want. It's that the competing external viewpoints become louder than their own inner voice. The advertisements on every website telling you they have the perfect solution. Leading a team of hundreds where you want everyone's voice to count, and you end up with hundreds (or thousands) of opinions in a survey. How do you make aligned decisions when every decision seems mission-critical?

Barbara Fredrickson's broaden-and-build theory of positive emotions, which tested and studied the effects of positive emotions, found that joy leads to expanded neurological behaviors, including creativity, pushing limits, and the urge to play. Most interestingly, it found that an increase in joy leads to "increased personal resources" defined as "pathways thinking, environmental mastery, self-acceptance, purpose in life, social support received, positive relations with others," which are all leadership skills for fostering trust and building team alignment.[1]

Joy builds the internal fortitude that fuels advancement. Positive emotions broaden your thinking, help you see more options, and, over time, build durable resources like optimism, problem-solving capacity, and social connections. This is the psychological "infrastructure" you need to take on bigger opportunities.

Save time and reduce stress by letting joy lead. Leverage joy as your greatest tool, a decision-making functionality, not simply a feeling. Your learned and lived experiences prepared you for more than you realize. You are overtly over-qualified for your role and to make the types of decisions you're faced with. You have taken the time to get to know your team. You are ready to make decisions rooted in joy. Leveraging joy as your compass empowers you to explain less, as the decision will easily integrate with the team's work, how you run your household, or your budget. Your mind and body feel at ease after you make the decision. Mental negotiation with yourself comes to a halt when you lead with joy.

When joy is missing, decisions feel heavy. When joy is present, decisions feel clearer, even when they're hard.

This is not a method about vision boards. This is a method about vision and goals.

The doorman buzzed me up. I walked into the common area of my friend's building overlooking the beautiful

Lake Michigan, and although it was pitch dark outside, the lake always has a calming effect, as you can't see where it ends. It feels like endless possibilities.

There was a giant table with chairs around it. She'd ordered pizza and prepared beverages for us all to enjoy. I didn't know anyone other than my friend who was hosting. The table was full of magazines and glue sticks, and one section had giant white poster boards.

The room was toasty, and we all chit-chatted as we flipped through the magazines to pick out what would go on our poster boards. It's almost like instant intimacy as we dove right into sharing our dreams, flipping through magazines in search of a resemblance...a photo, a graphic, a logo...anything that felt like what we were searching for. We shared what we were looking for with each other in case someone else saw it while flipping through.

As I flipped through the pages, I felt nothing—blank and empty. I enjoyed the conversations; however, I didn't enjoy searching the magazines for a resemblance to my future. The contents of the magazines just didn't quite feel real to me.

As more people arrived, I saw Kaitlin come in and begin to pull additional magazines from her purse. I heard our hostess's excitement and wanted to see what Kaitlin brought.

There it was. There I was. Finally.

Kaitlin brought magazines that primarily featured photos and imagery of Black people—Black women, Black children, Black families, Black men, etc. She simply shared that she thought we might want these. She was right! I didn't even know what I needed until she whipped those magazines out of her purse. In order to see myself in the vision I'd be putting on the board, I needed to see *myself* (not anyone else).

At the end of the evening, we each presented our poster boards and explained what each magazine clipping represented. I remember some of their dreams, some of their names...and I've seen some of their dreams come true by way of LinkedIn posts, but honestly, I barely remember names, dreams, or even faces...even though I wish I did.

Popular tools work for some but might not work for everyone.

Vision boarding quickly became a popular approach to goal crushing that is widely known and understood. In theory, it makes sense, but in activation, you might uncover gaps in the approach, as it can be difficult to know what your next step is. Consider how often you've referenced your vision board, felt overwhelmed by the number of dreams on it, or forgotten about it altogether. Did you stay in contact with folks who were in the room when you created them for accountability?

If the input is distorted, the plan is distorted as well. Joy is a truth teller. It reveals what matters.

External validation will have you perpetually chasing perfection, which is exhausting. When creating the blueprint for achieving your dream-sized goals, you deserve a roadmap that accurately reflects who you are. Think of yourself as a luxury car that requires premium unleaded gasoline. If you put regular unleaded in your tank, you get poor performance; whereas, when you put premium unleaded in, you get optimal performance. That's how your goals are; misaligned inputs lead to misaligned outputs. Sure, you can get away with regular unleaded for a while, but eventually you want your car to perform better.

In goal crushing, the differentiator from external noise and internal truths is joy. You can leverage your inner joy as a car would premium unleaded gasoline. When joy becomes your compass, you can achieve anything you put your mind to.

Imagine a goal-crushing method focused on your internal truths rather than external validation. A method that creates space for you to lean on your internal joy and create an aligned vision for your life with supporting goals. Goals that are not overwhelming and build on each other over time. Something you can legitimately move forward with.

This book is about leveraging your joy to build your dream life and how to stop paying attention to all the "shoulds" in life.

The Vision and Goals Method™ was initially designed to go deeper, as I truly want to see you build a life you currently can only imagine. Leading with joy propels you to amplify it in a way that feels real and aligns with your dreams.

DEFINING JOY

Writing this book, the hardest concept for me was finding the balance of what to share about my own joy and my clients' joy, as I fundamentally believe that we don't need a clone of me or anyone else. We need a mix of people with different joy factors who are living them out loud. I was nervous that if I talked too much about my joy, it would become the rubric, which is the opposite of my purpose in sharing this book. I intend to share tools to help you tap into your unique joy, nurture it, and protect it.

Look deep within. This is the fascinating part, and the difficult part is that no two people are exactly alike.

You might wonder if it's the lack of something, the addition of something, or something else altogether, along with where joy is located.

And you might think something like peace is a universal joy, but I was recently surprised. I met a woman who told me she "thrives in chaos" because she loves solving problems. It was fascinating to hear her talk about different times of turbulence and how she handled them. I watched her body language ignite as she shared how she navigates difficult times. She literally gets joy from thriving in chaos.

I don't, but it stuck in my memory. And I know who to call when I have a big, tangled, messy challenge that feels like too much for me to see how to untangle.

Joy is not universal. It's not something that is the same for each of us, and that's the most beautiful part about joy. You get to define your joy.

In 2025, I keynoted a conference that I'd spoken at in a thirty-minute breakout session the previous year. There was an attendee, Daryl Anne, who really got it! After the keynote, she found me and shared that last year, she was so happy to learn about joy-rooted goals and to remember that she deserves joy. And then this year, it layered on with now that you have goals grounded in your joy, you can be clear with those around you and build the right community for yourself. I was elated to hear how Daryl Anne described it because although the topics can be done as stand-alone, they are truly concepts/methodologies that build upon the previous ones, and all have joy at their source.

It takes me back to Fredrickson's research, as it showed that joy doesn't lead directly to better relationships. First, you experience joy, which "broadens feelings of warmth and caring toward others," then that leads to "building personal resources." The key step is activating joy within yourself, as it enables you to develop deeper relationships with others.

When your goals are rooted in joy, you're more excited about them and accomplish them faster because they no longer feel like a mundane task to check off the list. When you're clear on your goals, you can build community more easily, as it comes naturally since you have goals and joy factors you're excited to talk about. Then, once you have joy-based goals and a network that supports them, you're ready to be a leader who helps others succeed. Expanding to leadership is the third phase of The Stay Joyful Method, and I'm looking forward to hearing Daryl Anne's perspective on it.

Think about it for a minute.

Can you truly lead without first building community? And can you build community without clarity? The quickest way to clear objectives is through your lens of joy.

This is why I am building the business case for joy by teaching teams how to leverage it as a strategic advantage for goal setting, networking, and team alignment.

My clients are experiencing great wins by leveraging my joy-based methodology, and my hope is that you will experience the same 'aha' moments, combined with actionable steps, through this book.

WHAT IS YOUR JOY?

Joy is your compass for decision-making, creating an aligned roadmap for your life.

What I mean by joy in this book is your ultimate data source for being strategic with your choices. Your joy is unique to you, built over time through a culmination of your past experiences, both formal and informal. It acts as a Swiss Army knife in that you can use it to guide you in various situations.

Joy is not what the world is pressuring you to think it is. The pre-written story of what a "successful life" looks like may not bring you joy. It may actually even bring you stress. You deserve to focus on inner joy instead of worldly expectations.

When is the last time someone asked you what brings you joy? It's not a common question because we've been trained to focus on safe, surface-level conversation starters like "How's work?" or "How's your family?" or "How's school?" or "How's dating?"

Those questions are all so specific that they box you into thinking about those success measures as the thing you chat about. When you ask what brings someone joy, it leaves the conversation open to any and everything that might bring them joy. Your conversation starter shifts to endless possibilities rather than limiting assumptions.

Saying goodbye to worldly expectations signals a hello to your inner joy.

As you shift to this mindset, you'll begin to engage in conversations differently, excited about your own joy and curious about others'.

As exciting and wonderful as joy is, it can also be scary and land you in unknown territory. Coming to these exercises with the frame of mind that you deserve joy is helpful.

If this feels hard, you're not broken. You may need support. Coaching helps build forward; therapy helps you heal backward. This book is a method; it is not meant to replace care.

Starting With Joy

Joy, as a foundation for living life, will take you further than you ever imagined. It will take you around the globe and back again.

Starting with joy means that, even in the hard times, you'll persevere, knowing you're working toward something personally meaningful to you and your life. Joy is the most powerful tool in your toolkit. No matter what your job is—entry level to C-suite, blue collar to white collar, corporate to nonprofit to government—across the board, joy makes the people around you happier about their workday and leaves a lasting impression.

I believe we deserve joy, and I believe joy is not limited to one area of your life.

Joy Works

In the BCG Henderson Institute's Making Work *Work* survey, they found that two of the biggest blockers when people don't have joy are a lack of motivation to stay at the company and a sense of feeling unsupported. "Employees who enjoy their work are 49% less likely to be looking for outside employment."[2]

The intersection of joy and decision-making is grounded in rigorous neuroscience and produces measurable organizational outcomes. When individuals make decisions aligned with what brings them joy, they activate specific neural pathways that enhance cognitive processing, broaden creative thinking, and build lasting resilience.

The question I will mirror back to you throughout this text is, "What brings you joy?" It's different for everyone, so I cannot tell you your exact joy factors. If you find yourself stunned by this, just know I've been there, too: wanting to be told the answer rather than discovering it for myself.

JOY JUMPSTART

Write down five things that come to mind if I asked, "What brings you joy?" Focus on the first things that come to mind. Be mindful not to concern yourself with cost, feasibility, or other matters. You can figure those out later, but if you don't name your joy, there won't be anything for you to figure out.

CHAPTER 2

Plan From Joy, Not Pressure

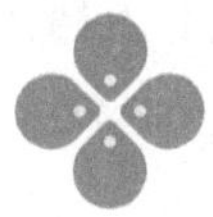

Nobody plans to fail at achieving their goals. It's not about discipline either. They simply don't have a framework for setting and achieving goals that align with who they are as a person and as a leader. There is a lot of pressure to be perfect, but not enough space to pause and be yourself. Be mindful of the pressures as they can distract you from creating goals rooted in your joy. When writing a goal down on paper, if you feel like you're writing it to make someone else happy or as though it's the "right" thing to do, you might be succumbing to pressure rather than joy. On the other hand, when writing a goal that's rooted in joy, you will feel motivated by the goal regardless of how difficult it is to achieve. Pressure is the "shoulds" of the world; whereas, joy is the alignment that actually works for you.

With the Vision and Goals Method™, you're not looking at outer worldly expectations by clipping magazine photos of someone else's world, which is manufactured marketing. Instead, you're getting up close and personal with your own unique joy by taking time to dig deep and define it for yourself, which, admittedly, can be scary if you're not ready to confront yourself on an introspective journey.

With the Vision and Goals Method™, you're building a road map or, as I like to call it, an attainable life strategy. It's broken up into smaller attainable goals, making them feel doable rather than stressful.

5-STEP VISION AND GOALS METHOD™

The major difference between the Vision and Goals Method™ and other goal-setting processes is that this system is designed to support you now and into the future. This system is built to grow with you as you evolve over the years and to celebrate your milestones rather than simply brushing by them. It is centered on your unique joy factors to empower you to build a life unlike anyone else's. Implementing this system is a mindset and lifestyle shift where you'll create a bespoke roadmap toward your dream life.

Joy moves with you through each step as your personal compass. It is important to go through steps one through five in order, as they strategically build upon each other.

Step 1: Energize Your Mindset

First, meditating. The world brings so much to you every day from all different directions. And you're full of "shoulds" which are what others impress upon you for your life.

Start with meditation to help you clear your mind and calm your psyche so it's no longer in a state of rushing from one thing to another. You want to come toward joy with a sense of calm and peace, not a sense of hurriedness.

Start with a meditation to help you clear your mind. It serves as a sacred space to quiet the external noise that surrounds us all. Whether it be emails, TV, social media, to-do lists, friends, family, etc., we need to silence it first in order to make space to truly hear our own thoughts more clearly.

Meditate, quiet the outside world/noise, and turn inward. Use this time to shut out all of your thoughts from the day that are swirling around your head. All the external noise and to-do lists can wait. This is a moment to center yourself and calm your spirit.

Sometimes you need a purposeful pause. There are various types of meditation you can choose from. If this is your first time meditating, try a gratitude meditation to live in the moment. Close your eyes and as you take slow inhales, focus on one thing you are grateful for. Then, as you exhale, release what is making you feel stuck.

Continue with this pattern of gratitude inhales and release exhales for a few breath cycles. Embrace a sense of gratitude for who you are, the body that you have, the mind that you have, and be grateful that you have taken time out of your day to think about yourself, because that's not something that people do all the time. Life is chaotic and busy, so you don't always make time that is purely for yourself. This time for yourself is sacred. During this first step, you get grounded and rooted with yourself.

Take your pause whenever you need it, for however long you need. You can come back to step one anytime, any day, or any moment. I recall from my journal that there was a full year when I focused on pausing deliberately to prepare for a major pivot. It helped me slow down and not rush through getting clear on how I wanted to pivot.

While you are pausing, remember that it's a time to learn to sit in stillness with yourself and your thoughts.

We don't always need an extended pause, so remember you can take micro-pauses anytime throughout your day. Something as simple as stepping away from your computer for five minutes, taking a five-minute walk, doing a few stretches, taking a nap, or doing something else that offers you calmness.

So often we think it has to be a big production, like a sixty-minute yoga class or meditating for an hour. The truth is, these micro moments can sustain you even more.

Keep in mind, this first step of calming your mind and psyche is crucial, as it prepares your mind and body for the next steps.

Step 2: Recognize Your Joy

After you've made space for your own thoughts by quieting external distractions, move to step two of recognizing your joy.

Talking about joy and creating space to encourage people to discuss what brings them joy isn't the norm. For some, the answer to this question comes very quickly, and for others, it takes a moment to think it through. Both are okay, so take your time and explore your inner thoughts. If you need to use these journal prompts to help get your thought process going:

The last thing I laughed really hard at was ______________________.

Something that always makes me smile is ______________________.

I get excited to work on______________________.

When I'm ______________________, I feel happy.

Reminder: I'm not talking about what social media or the world is telling you is joyful. It may not be flashy items or something that makes someone else happy.

This is what's going to bring *you* joy (not anyone else). In this second step, I implore you to intentionally go introspective. This step lays the foundation for the remaining steps, as your true joy serves as your compass.

Step 3: Visualize Your Future

Everything builds on each other and also gets a little bit more intense.

After you've taken time to clear your mind in meditation and get serious about your unique joy, visualizing your dream life comes next. Think about who you are in ten years.

What is your dream life, and how is it connected to the joy you named? How does it amplify your joy?

It works best when you write in the present tense as if you are there now and start with the phrase, "I am XX years old." After that, write down everything you are in ten years. Imagine who you are in ten years, who you want to be in your life, and where you are physically in ten years. Ground this in what you wrote down about your joy.

Here's an example. If I were writing mine right now, I would say, "I'm fifty-one years old, and I have homes on two continents. My husband and I have children who have their own hobbies. I'm doing three speaking engagements a month. I sit on the board of a nonprofit that builds Black generational wealth. I've started The Stay Joyful Method certification program where other people are spreading joy using my methodology. I take at least four vacations per year, one with myself, one with my husband, one with my husband and kids, and one with my friends."

This is who I will be at fifty-one, and writing it in the present tense psychologically shifts things in your mind. Starting with naming your age makes your brain go "Oh wow. That's how old I am in ten years!" It makes it feel more tangible.

You can always start over again. Be mindful not to be your own worst critic, or to tell yourself it's too late or that you didn't accomplish a dream on time.

You didn't get married on time. You didn't have kids on time. You didn't finish college on time. You didn't make partner at your firm on time. You didn't make it to six figures on time. You didn't...you didn't...you didn't...but what about what you *did*?

This is your moment to dream differently. When you dream a dream rooted in joy, it is more concrete, and you can build a plan around it.

Starting with your own personal joy factors empowers you to dream outside of the box. When worldly expectations influence you, it is hard to think outside the box of what you "should" be doing, but when you take time to look deep within yourself, you won't even remember there's a box to consider staying within.

Step 4: Conceptualize Your Path

The next step, which is more of a brain stretch, is breaking your vision up into goals.

This step is deliberately about you as an individual, understanding that your joy has value. And you deserve to amplify it. That's why we meditate to drown out external noise; then we start with joy and craft our vision.

The understanding that you're a whole person, not siloed competing parts, is imperative to your growth and goal-crushing.

In a corporation, people need to understand that you will have professional goals and KPIs, but you will also have personal, health, and financial goals.

This was pivotal for me because when I was younger, I went really hard at work because all I could think was "I gotta make it."

When I started understanding that I needed goals in other areas, I began to see how they came together to make the whole me. Therefore, it amplified my overall joy. That's why this step is important.

Take your vision and break it down into long-term, mid-term, and short-term goals so you have a road map. Write out your ten-year, five-year, and one-year goals in each of the four key areas of life (personal, professional, health, and financial).

Start with the ten-year goals that are closely related to your ten-year vision. After that, write your five-year goals, which are where you need to be at the halfway mark. Last, write down your one-year goals, which are the small, attainable steps you can start doing today to support achieving your long-term goals.

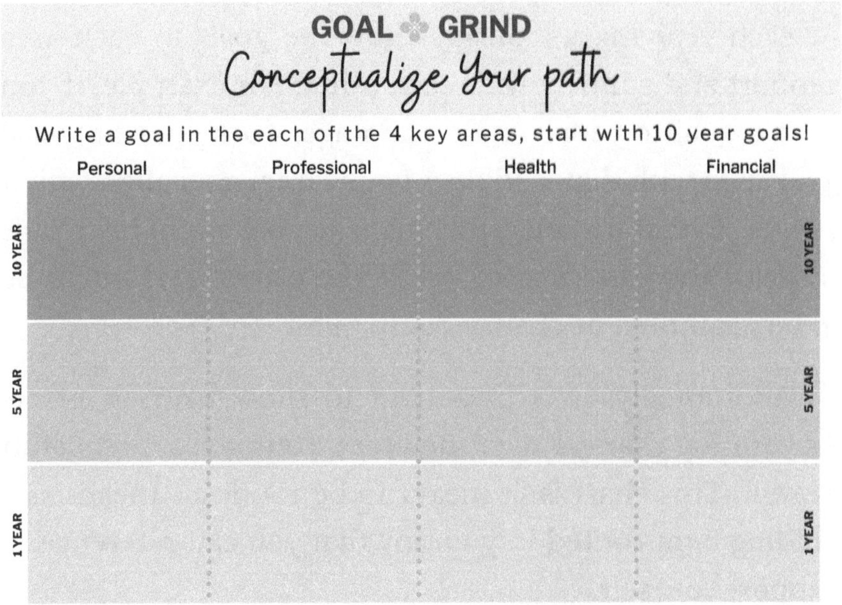

Short-term decisions lead to long-term success. It's called a Conceptualization Chart because you're conceptualizing your life over the next ten years and saying to yourself, "If my vision is this, where do I need to be in ten years personally, professionally, health-wise, and financially?"

Then, taking each of those and saying, what's the half-way mark? What's at five years, and what does that look like in five years?

Then, what can I do today and this year to make steps toward my larger goals?

This is your bespoke roadmap to your dream life. At each year mark, consider how the goals in each area support and connect with each other. For example, if you have a goal to retire at a certain age, does your financial goal align with that, and does your career goal align with it as well? In that instance, the financial goal might be to save more or increase income, while the career goal might be to be promoted or change companies.

Additionally, it is important to show yourself grace. As your joy changes over the years, your goals might shift as well. This chart isn't meant to be rigid; it's meant as a guiding light rooted in your joy that you can reference to support yourself.

Consider this observation.

Vision board = dreams only

Vision and goals = dreams with plans to get there

Your Conceptualization Chart is like a vision board with strategy, enabling your confidence and clarity to achieve these giant goals.

It is important that, after you've envisioned your future in step 3, you speak your truth into it in this step, as you are in this plan.

We're going to dive deeper into the four key areas in a chapter 6, but for now, just keep in mind that they're all interconnected parts of you to form a whole.

Step 5: Realize Your Results

The final step is crucial as you think through how to crush these goals.

Think about where in your home you will post your Conceptualization Chart (your goals), and determine what support you will need to achieve them.

You need a place to put your goals. Find a place to post your goals chart so you can see them regularly. If you just shove it in a drawer and forget it, you won't think about them. My chart is in my closet because I love fashion, so I spend a lot of time there. I've had people share that it's going in their office or on their refrigerator. One really inventive person said they took a photo of theirs and set it as their phone's screensaver so they see it every time they use their phone.

You know yourself, and you know where you're most likely to see it as well as where you'll need to see it in times that you could use the inspiration to keep going. That's where you post your Conceptualization Chart of goals.

You need your people. Think about who is in your support system and what role they play. These are not general people; they're specific to your joy-rooted goals. You might find yourself with gaps in your support, so we'll talk about finding the right people to fill those gaps in later chapters.

Consider other types of support you'll need on your journey in joy. Perhaps there's an educational gap preventing you from achieving your goals, which you can add to your support list.

If you work best with accountability, include options that provide that support. Last, think about how you can attain the support you need.

When I was younger, someone told me that life is like sitting in a canoe going down a river, and you have two options. You can use oars to guide your canoe or let the current take you where it wants to. Ever since then, I've been a goal-driven person. I wanted to own my canoe and be in charge of where it was going! I wanted to take those oars and paddle with all my heart in a direction that makes me happy.

This method is about grabbing life by the oars and paddling in the direction you choose.

The Vision and Goals Method™ might sound like five simple steps, but it's actually very deep, introspective work.

At this point, I want to celebrate you for creating your first life strategy using the Vision and Goals Method™. This system isn't easy, and it will continue to stretch your mind. I implore you to take a moment to be proud of the investment in yourself that you made. Make note of how you feel after this mental workout and how you will make micro movements toward your goals.

Initially, I did these steps on my own (or, I guess, with my pup, Chanel) in our home. I would sit down and meditate, then, after meditating, I would think about my joy. I would write down what brings me joy and use that as the guiding light to build my vision. I hadn't created the Conceptualization Chart then, so I had notecards I'd write on and tape to the side of my dresser.

When I first started doing Vision and Goals Parties, they were at my home or at the home of women who hired me to lead their friends through one. The refinement of this system over time is my gift to you, which is why I have always collected data and included multiple Journeys in Joy within this text.

This system is how you crush goals with joy rather than burnout.

YOUR GROCERY LIST FOR LIFE

I like to compare creating your life strategy with the Vision and Goals Method™ to grocery shopping. When you go to the grocery store, starving and without a list, you haphazardly grab everything you see in the aisles and overbuy. You might even forget to pick up staple items like milk. It's hard to focus (because you have no focus). So why would you do this with your life? Why would you send a starving you to the grocery store without a list?

Making your grocery list for life looks like this:

1. You close your eyes and take a deep breath. That's your mind energizer.

2. You start with what sounds yummy and/or easy to make. That's your joy factor.

3. You move on to wanting to feed yourself and your family for a specific time frame. That's your vision.

4. You make a list for each recipe. Those are your four key areas.

5. You decide what grocery store you'll go to that has the ingredients for your recipe and who (if anyone) is going to the store with you. That's you getting support.

This is precisely what the Vision and Goals Method™ prevents: shopping for your life without a clear plan.

JOY JUMPSTART

Pick one of the four key areas of life (personal, professional, health, or financial) that you haven't spent much time thinking about goals for. Write down your ten-year goal(s) in this area, followed by your five-year goal(s), and then your one-year goal(s).

You might consider sharing these goals with someone you trust and can be vulnerable with. Think about who would be excited for your goals, even if they're not the same as their own goals.

JOY THAT CONNECTS YOU

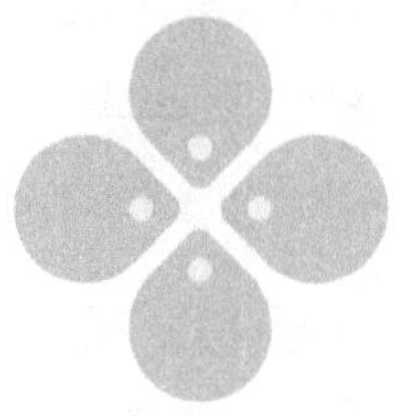

JOURNEYS IN JOY: THE WEALTH ADVISOR WHO LEARNED TO INVEST IN HIMSELF

I watched Edward walk into the Financial Services Pipeline conference laser-focused on one thing: his next achievement. Series 7. CFP. B-school. The letters after his name were multiplying faster than his joy was. He was brilliant, driven, accomplished, and utterly alone in it.

"I was definitely very career and goal driven," Edward admits. "I've always been kind of a 'what's next' career-focused person in terms of accomplishments and what I am able to do."

When he heard me speak about networking with joy, something shifted. Later, I was invited to lead a workshop at his company, and Edward finally asked himself the question no one had asked him before: What about you?

"When I laid out my goals, I would always lay out my professional goals."

Edward went on to share that I always followed up by asking him about his mental health, personal goals, and any goals he might have outside of work. He explained, "That's been a self-discovery journey in itself."

It challenged him to think beyond the boards he sits on and what he's doing when he's at home and takes off the suit.

He went on to tell me, "That's when I really knew that this was a different type of guided goal setting because when it comes to my professional life, I've never thought of me."

When it came to his personal and health goals, he had none.

So, Edward did something radical: He built a life. He got intentional about relationships, not networking dinners, but real connection. He started therapy. He picked up golf, yoga, and biking. He pursued a committed relationship. "I do want to have a family. I do want to be a father. I do want to be healthy."

But here's what nobody expects: The moment Edward stopped treating his personal life like an afterthought, his career accelerated. He passed his CFP exam. He got promoted to wealth advisor.

"It made me focus on myself a bit more. I've intentionally sought out things that help me relax and are specifically for me. I'm not doing it for anyone else, but I'm doing it for my personal joy," Edward explained.

"I've realized along the journey quality is not quantity, and you will burn out if you do not learn how to set aside time for yourself."

This is what joy that connects you actually looks like. You're going to read more about guarding what gives you clarity next and also learn, like Edward, that networking doesn't have to be performative.

Connection is about being with people who multiply your joy: a therapist, golf buddies, a partner who loves you. It's relationships you build intentionally, not transactionally.

Edward's closing wisdom says it all: "Love yourself more than anything. Nobody is going to love you more than you. Do not fall in love with the role. Do not fall in love with the money. Love yourself in all of your forms."

When Edward learned to invest in himself, everything else—his career, his relationships, his joy—compounded.

If he can do it, so can you! Today, Edward is a CERTIFIED FINANCIAL PLANNER® and wealth advisor in the financial services industry. He's active in his community and proving that the best career moves happen when you finally connect the dots in your own life.

PART II

CHAPTER 3

Guard What Gives You Clarity

I use intentional language to describe joy. I am all about joy, and everyone around me knows it's my mission to spread joy to the world...a mission I take very seriously.

When your goals are rooted in your joy, you achieve them faster than anyone would ever imagine because you're more excited about them. You know that you're in the process of amplifying your joy by achieving your goals. This is the experience my clients and friends have had over the last fifteen-plus years. I've had it my entire life, but only more recently realized that it was something that had to be defined and shared.

JOY IS OUR OFFENSE AND OUR DEFENSE

Once you have your joy defined, nothing can stop you. Your joy becomes your offense and your defense.

Your offense, so you're ready for anything life throws your way. Your defense, shielding you as you go into the battles of life.

When someone asks why you're doing something, you immediately know why. It's because your joy led you there. It's a very satisfying position to be in. When naysayers would question why I was moving to Chicago or why I aimed to change careers, I knew my why was rooted in my joy, so their questions and/or comments about what I should be doing didn't faze me.

Take me for example, people often ask why I don't have a car and assume I don't know how to drive. It's actually not anywhere near that complex. It's simple. I don't like driving, so I have chosen to live in a city where I don't need to have a car to get around. I grew up in Oklahoma, where public transportation is basically nonexistent, so I very much know how to drive, as it was my only means of transportation for the first thirty years of my life. I even know how to drive a stick shift car, which isn't very common. I could buy a car if I wanted to, but then my budget wouldn't align with my joy, plus I'd be spending money on something I hate doing—spending a lot of money on it, actually. You might not relate to my exact experience, but you know the feeling of being misunderstood for wanting something different than most.

What I've realized is that not many people find a way to eliminate the daily things in their lives that detract from their joy, but I do. Driving gives me anxiety and makes me angry. Yes, I'm a full-fledged road rage girlie. I don't like that, and it doesn't bring out the best in me, so I got rid of it. On the contrary, I love walking around and experiencing the city each day because it never fails to bring me a new surprise. I love people and people watching, which I get a ton of by walking, using public transportation, and taking ride shares. I understand this lifestyle isn't for everyone, but I also don't care because, for me, it's important to honor my joy by spending my resources (time and money) to increase my joy and decrease my stressors. Not having a car and the related expenses have allowed me to shift those funds to things that bring me joy, like spending more on housing and vacations.

This is a simple, low-stakes example, but just imagine applying this to higher-stakes areas of your life. You can literally save a lot of money if you align your spending habits with your own unique joy factors. It will even help with the dreaded FOMO because when you know your joy, you don't feel like you're missing out when something brings someone else joy. Instead, you're simply happy for them to live in their joy while you live in yours.

It is time to claim and re-claim our joy...because if not now, then when?

PART II

Grounding your decisions in joy brings a sense of calm to your mind and body, as you are more assured of your decision and understand why you made it. It replaces your doubts from misaligned choices with clarity and alignment. You will save yourself time and energy that can be spent on other tasks, thus increasing overall productivity.

When you live with increased clarity, it becomes harder to return to a time of internal uncertainty. Naturally, you'll begin to protect your joy at rising levels as you recognize its power as the root of your decision-making compass.

This is why I have the utmost respect for my joy as well as others' joy. It is a powerful tool when you tap in and really use it.

What we see and who we're around regularly have a significant impact on our lives. Initially, you might think this only pertains to the people physically in your presence, but it's more than that. It's your digital presence, too. We all, me included, have felt the pain of social media faux-perfectionism. It's aggressive. The filters, the always "perfect" people, the faux experts, and the list goes on. This is why 99% of the time, I don't use filters. It's very surprising to me when people meet me in person and say, "You're exactly like your online profile!" I didn't understand this at first, until I realized how little people were like what they portray online. I am who I am because I am rooted in my joy, and my joy is what drives me, so there's no room to filter it.

THE JOY BUBBLE

When I set out to change my career from the non-profit to the corporate sector, people told me it would take at least ten years. I did it in under three.

When a manager told me I couldn't be promoted because company policy required a certain amount of time in a role, even though they acknowledged I had the skills, I went out and got a job at another company.

I let my joy lead, and I simply do not accept the rules. It wasn't malicious. It was me being about me and my joy, the greatest act of loving myself and knowing my self-worth.

There might be rules, regulations, and all sorts of red tape that take things away from you, but joy—joy will always and forever be yours. Tap into that! It's a powerful thing to leverage.

Typically, your day is filled with thinking about everybody but you. Maybe you're thinking about your team, thinking about your family, thinking about your friends, etc.

Joy Bubble time is a time to think about you and only you. Try to put yourself in the mode of "I don't care what anybody else thinks."

This is a great exercise for when you've just meditated, worked out, or done another relaxing activity, and you need to focus on yourself. When you're calm and relaxed, take out a piece of paper. Draw a circle on it.

In that circle, write down everything and anything that brings you joy. It can be things from any of the four key areas of life (personal, professional, health, and financial).

Don't think too hard on it. Set a five-minute timer and free write whatever pops into your mind first.

Once you've identified what brings you joy, USE IT!!! Use it to set your goals, make decisions, and celebrate your wins.

It sounds simple yet can be a stretch if we're not used to thinking about our own joy. So, try it now for yourself. You started this exercise in the Joy Jumpstart of chapter 1, and now you're expanding it.

Selfishness

When you're completing this exercise, it's all about YOU! This is your time to be selfish...definitely not selfless, as I'm sure you do enough of that. We aren't usually told to be selfish, but right now, I want you to try really hard to only care about you and your joy. So, not what you want to do for your teammates, family, or friends, but instead what you want for you if no one else were around. What would you choose if you were the only decision maker? What would you choose if money were no object?

It's not often that somebody says to you, "What brings you joy?" That's why this step is crucial.

While you're writing, keep in mind that this can (and will) change, so don't pressure yourself toward perfection. We are all growing humans, which means our joy grows and changes with us. I set my own vision and goals at least once a year, which means I return to this step each year to reflect on what brings me joy.

I love this exercise because it's truly the foundational piece of everything I teach.

When I put everyone into groups during workshops to share their joy factors, it sparks deeper conversations as folks are intrigued by learning what makes each other experience joy.

Then, when the small-group time concludes, and people decide to share with the full group, I'm always intrigued by what's shared, as it's truly unique to each individual, and I hear different responses each workshop.

Giving the Gift of a Joy Bubble

Often, when I meet people who are feeling lost or ask how I found my joy, I respond with "My gift to you is joy."

I go on to share with them that joy is the greatest tool in their toolkit of life. It's a resource that can be used in various ways. It's the decision-making compass that creates an aligned roadmap for your life.

In short, what I give them is the simple present I created: the Joy Bubble.

I go on to give them a brief explanation of how to create their Joy Bubble. When I tell people this, they get excited to do it. I let them know it will empower them: You can see it, touch it, and feel it. And anytime you're having a stressful moment or a bad day, take out your Joy Bubble and do something from it.

For example, yoga is in my Joy Bubble. So when I'm in the midst of stressful times, I might do a quick breathing exercise like box breathing, where I inhale for four, exhale for four, and hold it. If that's not your jam and that's not in your Joy Bubble, don't do that because we're trying not to "should" on other people's lives. (Remember, the introduction covered the importance of not "shoulding" on people.) I can tell you my examples, but that might not necessarily be what brings you joy.

Our pathways inevitably have unexpected turns and twists, but joy is the filter you can leverage to ensure those turns and twists don't distract you from achieving the goals you set forth for yourself.

Imagine you have a clear career plan, and then the company you work for loses a major contract, which is the source of funds that pay your salary. That is a major distraction in your plan if you enjoy your role and had no plans to alter that portion of your life. Take out your Joy Bubble and consider what you enjoy about your role (and what you don't enjoy about it) to guide your path as you begin to explore options. Having your Joy Bubble enables you to do this more quickly than your teammates who haven't spent time exploring their joy, becoming as grounded in their truth. Focusing on your joy enables you to be nimble in times of unexpected change, as it is your reminder that you do, in fact, have choices even when it is hard to imagine what those choices might be.

Joy is a choice that can be difficult to make and difficult to recognize that you deserve it. I choose my joy by understanding it and making time for it. I refresh my Joy Bubble at least once a year, meaning I spend time sitting in silence with myself and writing down exactly what brings me joy. Some things stay the same, and some change, but the important thing is that I'm acknowledging my joy.

When I give people the gift of the Joy Bubble, I also instruct them to refer to it on bad days. We will all have bad days, but imagine what it would be like to work through them if you already have a Joy Bubble? That's when you go to your Joy Bubble and identify something you can do for yourself. It can be small and simple or large and extravagant. The only thing that matters is that it was in your Joy Bubble and you're doing it for you. Choosing joy isn't something that happens overnight. It's a lifestyle choice that you must commit to, nurture, and renew regularly.

Choosing joy will impact every area of your life—personal, professional, health, and financial. The choice for joy enables you to go further and build deeper.

Life is hard, which is why choosing joy isn't the easy route. On the surface, it sounds like it is, but it's actually the harder one. When I have hard days, my first instinct isn't to get my Joy Bubble. I have to remind myself, which is why my Joy Bubble is somewhere visible in my home. Also, knowing my joy has determined who is in my joy squad, and they're able to remind me of my joys and how I live for them. The hard days are when I need my cheerleaders the most.

JOY JUMPSTART

Create your own Joy Bubble. Creating a Joy Bubble is your foundational compass that we will refer to throughout this book. You will inevitably add to it throughout your journey. I recommend that you keep it somewhere easily accessible that you'll remember, so you don't have to search for it.

PART II

CHAPTER 4

Build Community Without Performing

This chapter is about taking the ick out of networking and replacing it with purpose by coming from a place of joy. We're all awkward at some point. Use this strategy to go from awkward wallflower to intentional connection builder.

A PAUSE WITH PURPOSE MOMENT

I recently realized, through conversations, that some of the most amazing, talented, and successful women in my life didn't see themselves. I invite you to pause with purpose. The thing is, we need to pause, reflect, and celebrate our own accomplishments...without guilt or shame.

You worked hard to get where you are, and you're working hard to go where you're headed. You deserve to be seen by others, but more importantly, by yourself. For if we don't recognize what we've built...we won't be able to help others build.

I'm clapping for you! The question is, are you clapping for you?

I often get asked how I got so clear on my purpose, which is why I'm looking forward to sharing that with you in this chapter. I took time to think through how I found my purpose and how I've grown it over time, with a sense of gratitude mixed with a profound and deeper understanding of self each day.

ELEVATOR PITCH AND BEYOND METHOD

Step 1: Discover Your Purpose

The four steps of the Elevator Pitch and Beyond Method are also ordered in a progressive fashion, starting with purpose as the starting point for networking and building true community with others. When you understand your purpose, you have a sense of clarity that empowers those you meet to become excited about what you're doing, curious about how you're doing it, and wanting to support your journey in joy. You become a magnet for the exact type of community you need and thirst for.

Imagine meeting someone, and as you listen to them, you feel their energy and pure joy as they communicate with you. It has a sense of clarity that makes it click for you. That's when you become intrigued and ask questions. This is why making time to become clear with yourself is the first step of networking with joy.

Return to your Joy Bubble as the foundation for this exercise. Take it out and keep writing what brings you joy. You might not have included many things from work last time, so consider adding what you do at work that gets you super amped up. Consider what you are really good at doing that you have so much fun at that you'd do for free, even though others find immense value in it.

For me, it's building strategies. I love building strategies! Nothing gets me more excited than making a master plan. It's nerdy. I know. But it's also who I am. I'm also very aware that I hate data engineering. I am data-minded; however, I do not want to be the data architect, figuring out what goes where and why.

This is why I excelled so much in my corporate roles. I was the one whom the leaders brought in when a major change needed to be made. I also love communicating with people over the phone, hearing them out, and chatting things out. Another skill I enjoy that has led to my corporate success is my ability to initiate change from a place of understanding, driven by my communication style and strategic thinking.

The point isn't about me having clarity. The point is what happens when you network from a place of clarity about your strengths and joys.

During my time at a global aerospace company, I was constantly in awe of a teammate who could master data and make it digestible for others. Gina was and will always be a data wiz...and she loves data. I remember when she taught me to do pivot tables, and my mind wasn't grasping it. She used to jokingly say "PIVOT!!!" to me in reference to Ross trying to get Rachel to turn when moving that couch up the flight of stairs on *Friends*. Rachel couldn't pivot the couch, and you know what...I can't pivot the data...and I hate it, which is why I was so glad to be partnered with a teammate like Gina, who not only had the skills but also the passion for data. She built the most beautiful dashboards that our entire team could use to easily pull data and share a fact-based story about our work. It was remarkable. Gina had stepped into *her* purpose.

StrengthsFinder is my favorite personality test because it identifies our natural talents, then it directs you to build a team with the opposite talents. You will inevitably encounter times in life when people want you to expand or branch out into areas you have no interest or skill in just because it will make you money. My question to you is, "Do you want to be miserable doing something all day, every day, because you couldn't figure out how to make money doing something you enjoy?" That's what ends up happening to so many people, and that's why the workday feels like an eternity instead of a moment.

Your Accomplishments Journal

Oftentimes, it's difficult to see our own accomplishments. To start out, write down what you're proud of accomplishing. Then, write down what your boss and/or teammates have recognized you for. Also, consider any awards you've received and what they were recognizing you for.

After you start this list, it's important to keep it updated. Set aside time each week to write down your accomplishments. This list is not only useful for this exercise but also for aggregating in preparation for performance reviews, on your résumé, and in interviews. It will help you be proactively prepared rather than reactively scrambling to complete your performance evaluation, update your resume, or understand how to share your value in an interview. This is your Accomplishments Journal, and similar to the Joy Bubble, it is a helpful tool to reference regularly.

Joy + Skills = Purpose

There are things we are good at: skills. There are things we like doing: joy. There are things that yield both: purpose. The equation is simple.

joy + skills = purpose

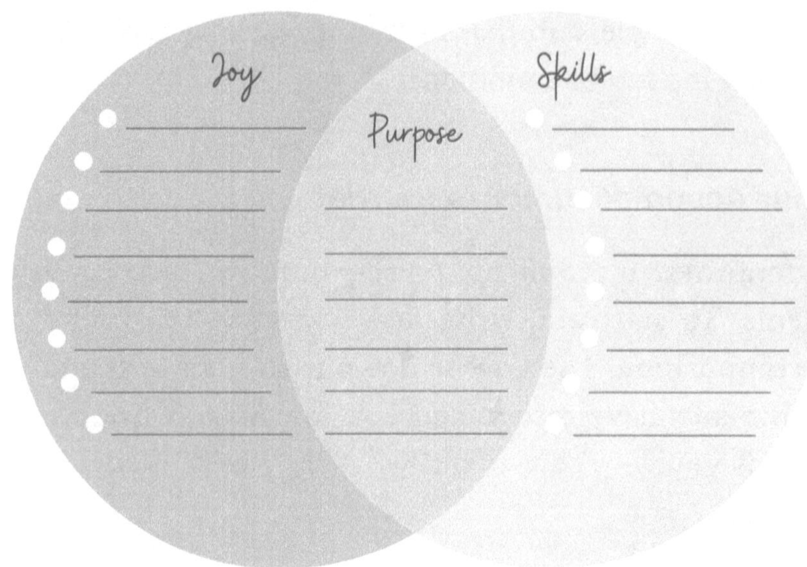

Anyone can learn to do a task, but the special sauce you add, which you and you alone can bring to the table? Those are your income-generating skills.

Keep in mind two things. One, not everything you enjoy needs to be monetized. Two, not everything you're skilled or good at do you enjoy enough to monetize.

The good news is that there are items at the intersection of your income-generating skills and your joy factors. Purpose emerges when your joy factors and income-generating skills collide.

Your ability to understand your purpose and clearly articulate it to others is what makes you a magnet for the community you will flourish within.

Clarity is kindness. The kindest thing you can do while networking is clearly and confidently share who you are and what your purpose is. People innately love to help one another; however, if someone doesn't know how to help you, they can't. When there is a lack of clarity, you get those awkward, "why are we here" or "why are we talking" silent thoughts and moments during events. You never connect with them in the future, as there is nothing of substance to connect about. Clarity is your key enabler, and the beauty is it's true and authentic to you; therefore, it doesn't feel performative.

Now imagine the next time you attend a networking event, you walk in with clarity and confidence to share your joy-centered purpose. Your conversations lead to exchanging information and quickly scheduling a call or meeting with the person to explore deeper synergies. This happens because both of you understand who the other person is and what your mission (or personal purpose) is. You have something to contribute to the other, where you can create a mutually beneficial relationship.

Your purpose is rooted in your joy. Your networking is rooted in your purpose; therefore, your ability to network authentically is directly correlated to your joy.

Step 2: Set Strategic Goals

Hint, hint. You've already done this! Return to your ten-year vision and your Conceptualization Chart, where you charted goals in the four key areas of life over ten-, five-, and one-year increments.

Let's look at the professional goals for this. What were they? What do you need to get to the next level in your career? Or what do you need to pivot to your next career?

When I did this the first time, I knew I wanted to leave the nonprofit sector and move into the corporate sector. To do that, I needed to learn about the field and expand my network there. This combination helped me validate my hypothesis that this is my dream job and helped me use vernacular as though I were already in the sector.

Keep in mind, career transitions are hard but not impossible. That's why imposter syndrome can start to come into play. When that happens, I want you to take out your Accomplishments Journal and read your wins out loud. It's important to hear yourself read them because it becomes more real than when you read it silently. Your wins are not silent...they're loud and proud so join them in being proud of YOU!

After reading your accomplishments, say this to yourself:

Imposter syndrome, be gone.

My Accomplishments Journal is proof that I'm that girl!

My 30-60-90 day plan is possible and executable!

My people believe in me, and I'm surrounding myself with positive people.

After speaking at a recent conference, I had a young lady ask me how to charge someone for her photography services. I looked her straight in the face and said, "You have to believe you deserve to get paid. I want you to look in the mirror every day and pump yourself up. Look in the mirror and say, 'You go, girl!'"

She cried, at which I was mortified until she told me she was crying because she appreciated being poured into so much. Then, of course, I started crying, too. I tell you this to say, you'd better cheer for yourself daily!

Affirming yourself might be one of the goals you need to work on in your journey to building your dream career. If it is, do it!

The clearer you are on your goals, the easier it is for others to jump in and support your glow up. The way you share your goals varies based on who you're talking to. Share long-term goals with your closest inner circle because they're in it for the long run and might have resources to support you long-term. Talk about short-term goals with your outer circle, as they're usually only able to take in small amounts and give quick tips for you to use immediately.

Quick reminder: Your goals are like you, always growing and evolving. It's okay if you need to add or subtract right now because you realize your professional goals don't support your purpose. You have more of the framework now. Beyond what you enjoy, we've added what you are also good at doing.

Now you have the tools to start thinking about what this looks like in practice. Additionally, think through how you can implement this practice in a way that resonates with you.

Step 3: Develop Your Professional Presence

Now that you understand your purpose and have strategic goals to support your purpose. Let's build your professional presence around it.

There are layers to this process. You can't begin to build a professional presence that serves your goals if you haven't set goals, and you can't set deep, meaningful goals unless you understand your joy factors. That's why there's an order to this practice.

Throughout this book, I like to remind you of our definition of *joy* as your decision-making compass. In this chapter, it's useful for creating an aligned roadmap to build toward your ideal job.

The first part of your professional presence is your elevator pitch. Think of this as how you share who you are in a way that makes people want to know more.

Before I realized there was a science to this, I always found networking events to be really fun because people would ask me more and more about myself. Now I know they were asking more because of how I initially shared about who I was, since it was always rooted in joy, which excited them.

As a hiring manager, I recall sitting in countless interviews where it seemed like the person was forced to be there. They weren't excited about the role or the work. They were just there. It was immediately refreshing when someone was not only excited about the work but also confident in their ability to do it. Those people were interviewing for jobs in their purpose sphere. Period.

Develop Your Elevator Pitch

Now, let's help you get a clear, joy-filled, and brief elevator pitch.

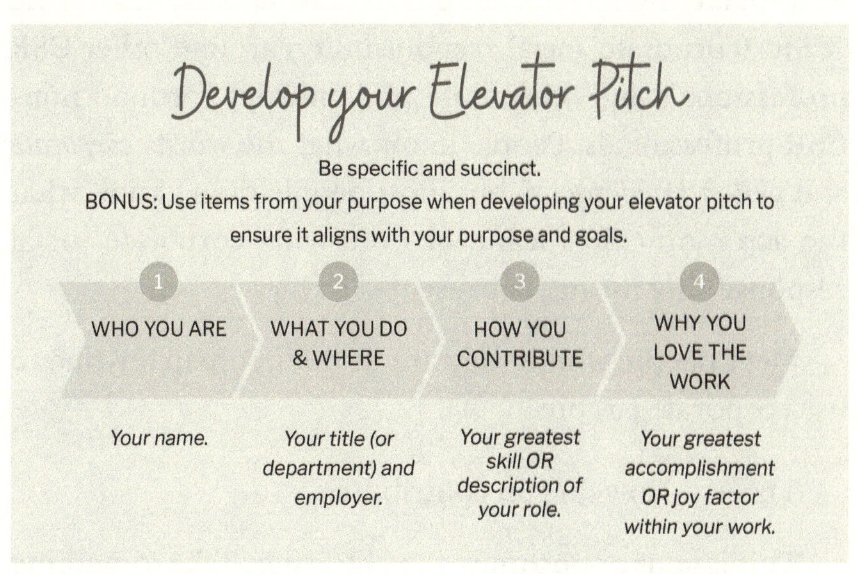

PART II

One – Who are you?

When writing this one, it's easy. It's your name.

Two – What do you do and where?

This is simply the company you're at and your title or department. Sometimes titles can be confusing or vary from company to company, which is why it can be good to simplify by using the department name. If both are complex, just go with a general term that is widely understood.

For example, when I worked at a global aerospace company, our team name was "Global Engagement," and I'm guessing that means nothing to you. When people asked me what team I was on, if I said, "Global Engagement," they'd give me a blank stare. That's when I started saying "CSR" (corporate social responsibility) around other CSR professionals and "corporate philanthropy" around non-CSR professionals. People know what the words *corporate* and *philanthropy* mean, but most people didn't know what the acronym CSR meant, or even what corporate social responsibility meant, because it is so niche.

Meet people where they are. It doesn't help anyone to use corporate jargon.

Three – How do you contribute?

This is your opportunity for a little flex. Take something out of your Accomplishments Journal and stick it here. Just one thing. No one has time for a list, and, furthermore, no one will remember more than one thing.

If you're multi-passionate, use what's applicable to the situation. For example, I have a friend who is a registered nurse and works full-time in that role. She's also a certified fitness instructor and has her own business teaching fitness classes. And third, she owns property and is a real estate maven. Imagine meeting someone, and they tell you they do all three of those at once. If you're like most people, you wouldn't know what to do with all of that, as you'd have stopped hearing anything after the first job title.

Instead, I advised her to shift based on the audience. When she's at a women in real estate event, she'll say that she's a property owner with properties across the Chicagoland region. When she's at the gym, she shares that she's a fitness instructor with contracts at the school district, helping teachers with their wellness so they can better serve students. While attending medical-related events, she talks about being a nurse.

See how that works? They are each true, but when used strategically, she empowers people to get interested enough to ask more, understand what she's talking about, and be enabled to support her through connections or collaboration ideas.

Four – Why do you love the work?

This is when you incorporate your joy factors! Show them your excitement, and they'll get excited, too, because enthusiasm is contagious.

Going back to data-loving Gina. When I'd talk to her, magically, I was excited about data, too, and that's the last thing I'd ever imagine being excited about. But it was the way she lit up and could convey data. She met me where I was and imparted wisdom to me by sharing.

Where Do You Use Your Elevator Pitch?

The great thing is that there are so many places where you can use this elevator pitch. You can use it

- At networking events

- In email introductions

- During interview introductions

- Within your LinkedIn about section

- On your personal website or online portfolio

And the list goes on and on. Wherever you need to be clear, concise, and strategic is where you'll use this.

Practice at your next networking event and pay attention to how people respond. Their facial expression of understanding or looking confused will tell you how clear and to the point you were. If they ask deeper questions or offer support, that is a good way to gauge whether you caught their attention. Taking note of these items will help you refine and fine-tune your elevator pitch over time.

Above all, be succinct and be confident.

Have you ever had someone call and say, "I saw this role and thought of you?" That's what you want people to think when they learn of a resource or opportunity that would be helpful to you in accomplishing your goal. The elevator pitch you give them, along with your goals, is what empowers them to take this action of supporting you.

Step 4: Build Your Personal Board of Directors

Your personal board of directors is the people who support your career advancement. There are five types of people you need for this, but you can seek out only four of them. The fifth one, sponsor, is a choice people make that you may or may not know that they made.

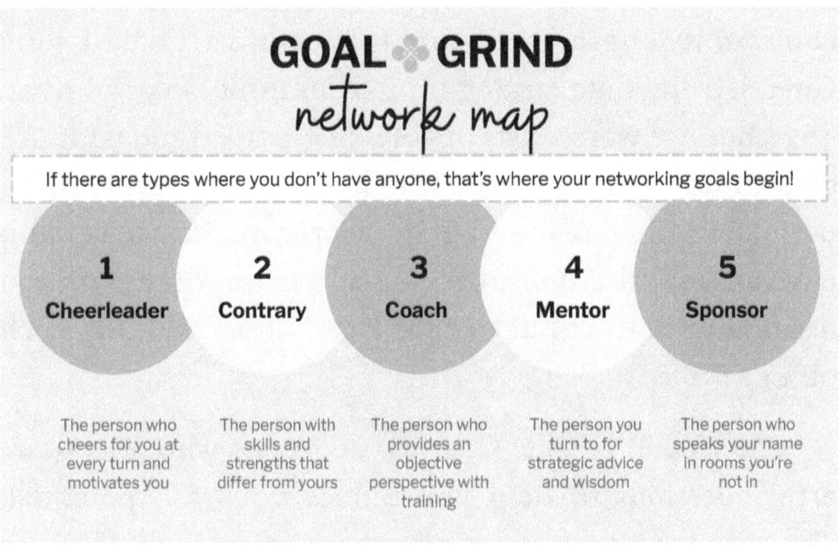

The Cheerleader – The Cheerleader is me! The person who motivates you and is cheering for your success. They might not know anything about what you're working on, but they know they believe in your ability to get it done! She's your ultimate hype girl.

The Contrary – The Contrary is one we don't always seek out but is a vital person in your personal board of directors. They're the person who thinks differently from you and has a different skill set than you. I'm more of a big-picture thinker and am not a data/numbers person. It's imperative that I have a data expert alongside my journey, as they think strategically about what data we need to collect and how the data will inform our future work. This type of person perfectly complements my skills by having opposing skills. When I worked at the global aerospace company, I led strategy for employee community engagement, and my teammate, data-loving Gina, led the data strategy for community engagement. Together, we were unstoppable! She helped me be more data-minded, and I shared with her the vision and implementation I had planned. Find people on your team who have an opposite skill from you and from whom you can learn. You both could benefit from understanding each other's skills.

The Coach – Your Coach is someone who asks powerful questions to help you unlock your full potential. The coach is like your sporting team coach in that they're pushing you. They don't have to have the same type of job as you or to have previously had the same type of job. Their role is to ask you curious questions that unlock your creativity and problem-solving capabilities. My business coach isn't a motivational speaker, corporate trainer, or author, even though those are my titles. He has owned a business before, but that's also not why he's a great coach. He's a great coach because he looks at my business plan and then asks very specific questions that bring me a plethora of aha moments. Think about who in your life is engaged with you and invested in your success by always asking you questions that inspire you and stretch your brain to consider new ideas.

The Mentor – Your Mentor is someone who has accomplished what you're trying to accomplish. They've been in your shoes at the starting line, which is why they can give you sage wisdom. They've been in your position before. This relationship is invaluable as you can learn from their mistakes. Ensure you have multiple people whom you can ask about their journey in joy.

The Sponsor – Your Sponsor is the person who champions you. They speak your name in rooms you're not in and might not have access to be in (but *they're* in those rooms)!

An example of this person is Bridget, my first boss at the global aerospace company. She called me one day and said that one of her contacts posted a job on LinkedIn that would be the perfect next step for me. She wanted to know if she could recommend me for the job. I said yes and began my interviews, nailed them, and landed my next great role at the world's number one CRM company. Now let's break down the importance of this sponsor. She knew me, my work, and my work ethic; therefore, she was confident she could recommend me. She was aware that I'd hit a growth plateau at the company where we met. She was selfless and made time to connect me with someone whose job was a good fit for me. None of this would have worked if we hadn't kept our relationship beyond her being my manager, and if I hadn't been clear with her on my accomplishments and aspirations. The point here is not that I got a new job. This is about the power of building mutually beneficial relationships within your network so you can support one another.

Who's Missing from Your Personal Board of Directors?

Maybe you have great cheerleaders, but you don't have a single contrary. Or perhaps you don't know anyone who's done what you're trying to do, so you need a mentor. Specifically, I mean someone you know in real life, someone you can pick up the phone and call anytime, who will answer questions for you. That's your mentor. It's not someone on TV, a podcast host, or an influencer because you don't have real access to those people. Your mentor is someone you can talk to about your specific situation, as each situation is unique, and you need to be advised on the specific complexities you're facing.

Don't forget to consider how you are perceived by others. As much as you deserve to be poured into, you cannot forget about pouring into others. Can you mentor those behind you? Are you being productive and collaborative with your teammates? Think about the last time you recognized a colleague for their success. Doing these doesn't have to be a major production. It can be as simple as sending an email to thank them for sharing their perspective in a meeting. It encourages them to engage in repeat behavior, to continue on the path that you appreciated, which shapes your relationship and builds trust.

How Do You Build Your Network, and Where Will You Build it?

There are so many spaces and places where you can build your network. It's exciting because you're likely already in those spaces. The question is, are you leveraging the spaces you're in to support your goals? That's the real question!

Think of five spaces you go to regularly where you interact with people. It doesn't need to be labeled as a networking event or a professional venue. Use the following chart as your rubric to fill in your network map.

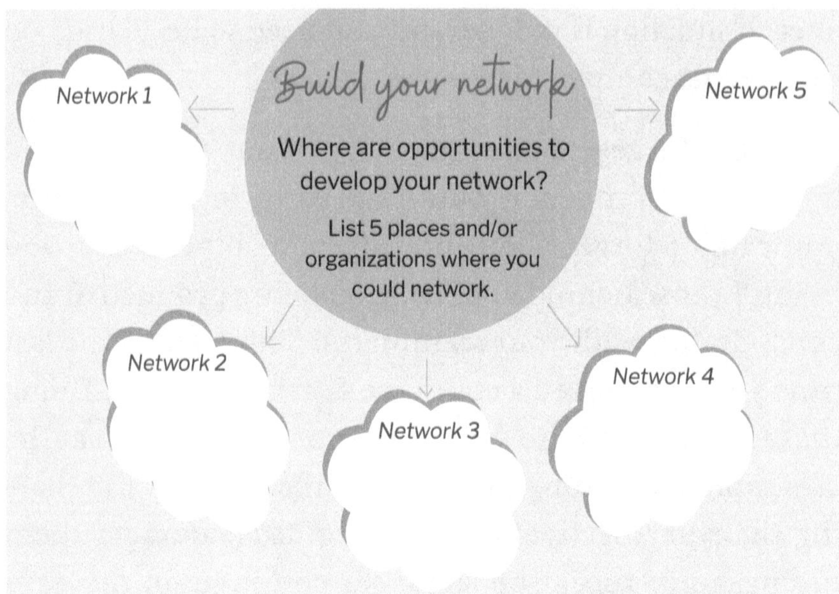

Some examples include volunteer groups, collegiate alumnae groups, health clubs, religious organizations, and Greek organizations. Certainly, include any industry-specific spaces, and keep in mind there can be opportunities outside of those. Start building your networking organizations list.

You never know when you're going to meet the person who changes your life. So be ready!

I was working a retail job when I first arrived in Chicago, and there was a woman who always came in. She was always clear about what she wanted, which I loved because it made it so easy to get her what she wanted.

One day she came in, and she said to me, "What do you want to do?"

I told her I wanted to pursue corporate social responsibility (CSR), and I was very clear about my why.

She said, "Okay. I have an introduction for you," and handed me her business card. It turns out she was a leader at a financial services firm, so she connected me with their CSR person, who then introduced me to the women in her network who did CSR. Those were the women who championed me, supported me, and spoke my name in rooms I wasn't in. They became my sponsors!

It was that simple. I reached out, and she made the introduction. That introduction led me to build my network of CSR professionals in Chicago, which would also help me secure my first CSR role at the global aerospace company.

Life has so many full-circle moments. Don't let your opportunities pass you by. Be ready and stay ready. It's truly beautiful and it all started with me working in a retail shop and having clarity on my next move.

If you've ever connected with someone, not knowing why at the time, but later supported them in some way, you understand where I'm coming from.

This all happened in alignment with what I'm sharing in this book.

My clarity came from my joy, as my vision and goals were rooted in joy. If it weren't for my being clear, I wouldn't have been able to answer her question in a way that enabled her to make the initial introduction. The initial introduction spun out to an entire group of women.

One moment of clarity can shift your world, too.

See how all the steps build on one another to build your joy-filled life? It's incredible when you really think about it. Which is why I'm sharing this with you!

PART II

JOY JUMPSTART

Write down your four-part elevator pitch. Call someone in your inner circle and share your elevator pitch with them. Ask them for their honest, unfiltered opinion as though they'd met you for the first time.

Ask specifically what caught their attention the most, what confused or distracted them, and what they found to be boring. Be sure you do this on the phone or video call so they can hear your voice (tone, inflection, etc.) and truly experience what it would be like for you to say it aloud to someone.

This practice will also help you become more comfortable networking with purpose, shed fears about delivering your elevator pitch, and identify any tongue twisters.

CHAPTER 5

Choose the People Who Multiply Your Joy

Your joy squad is your support network that helps you crush your goals, step into your purpose, and live your dream life. No two people in your joy squad do the same thing, as they're unique humans, too. The great part is that, together, they are exactly what you need. These are the people you trust, admire, and love.

You trust them to be honest with you as well as to be kind to you. You also trust them to keep your words confidential when needed, as you don't need every goal to be broadcast before you're ready for it to be shared publicly. You might just be running an idea by someone in your joy squad, and you need to be able to trust that they will keep it to themself. Take my journey, for example. When I was trying to decide if I'd move to Chicago and how I'd do it, there were people in my joy squad that I knew I could brainstorm different options with. Before I gave notice at my job, I had to understand my plan, and my joy squad helped me solidify it so I could quit with confidence and excitement rather than fear and doubt.

You admire them because you see how they move in their own life, and it aligns with the values you have for your life. Think about it for a moment. You wouldn't ask for advice from someone you don't admire because you wouldn't be able to trust it. I am so blessed to have a group of highly intelligent friends that I truly admire. Take my "lawyer ladies" as an example. When something goes left in my life, they are the voices of reason. They tell me the practical worst-case scenario and the legal worst-case scenario, which always calms my nerves because it's never nearly as bad as I thought it could be. After going through the worst-case legal scenario, they give me advice that I feverishly write down! Those are the calls that save the day in a crisis.

You love the members of your joy squad because you are also in their joy squad, meaning you support them and their goals. You are honored to be a trusted listening ear and an admirable confidant. You listen when they need a listening ear, strategize with them when they need a problem solver, and celebrate with them when they accomplish a goal. You love on them mentally and spiritually.

Share your goals with your joy squad. You can only support one another if you know what they need support with and how they best receive support. By boldly sharing your goals with your people (not just any people but your joy squad!), you develop additional layers of accountability and encouragement.

In the previous chapter, we explored how to build your personal board of directors, aka your professional joy squad. In this chapter, we'll explore how to identify gaps by auditing your circle, build by incorporating new people, and maintain relationships in your joy squads. We'll build the connection among the four key areas and have specific joy squads aligned with each. Each one serves a different purpose, and each is equally important to sustaining your joy.

A Joy Squad for Each of the Four Key Areas of Life			
Personal Joy Squad	**Professional Joy Squad***	**Health Joy Squad**	**Financial Joy Squad**
Accountability partners	Cheerleader	Medical team	Financial advisor
Travel friends	Contrary	Workout partners	Accountability partner
Family members	Coach	Wellness supporters	CPA/tax professional
Romantic partners	Mentor		Banker
Spiritual leaders	Sponsor		Bookkeeper
Value-aligned friends			Insurance advisor

*Your Professional Joy Squad is the same as your personal board of directors mentioned in chapter 4.

Your personal joy squad might be the most important of them all. It's your family and friends who are so close, they're your chosen family at this point. They're the people you call on, and they can call on you to support them as well. You engage with them most in your everyday life.

MULTIPLICATION VS. DEPLETION

When you spend time with people, their energy transfers to you and vice versa. Imagine every time you connect with someone, whether it be over the phone or in person, you always leave the conversation feeling uplifted in a positive way. You might not even remember everything that was discussed, but you know you want to interact with them again, as you want that energy.

On the contrary, think about the times you've interacted with someone, and you couldn't wait for the conversation to be over. You hung up the phone, thinking to yourself that you'd be okay never talking to them again. You feel exhausted after being in their presence. This is the difference between people who multiply positive energy and those who deplete through negative energy.

Access

Who gets the privilege of having access to you and your time? I use the word *privilege* intentionally, as throughout this process, you will notice a shift in understanding access to you as a privilege reserved for those who show respect for you and, therefore, deserve that access.

Your Bus of Life

Your life is a bus, and you're in the driver's seat! As the driver, you have decisions to make, including who belongs in the front seat, who's in the middle, who's in the very back, and ultimately who's getting dropped off at the next stop.

When the wrong people are on your bus, it will end up broken down on the side of the road with a smoking engine (or worse). Who are the people who will cause your bus's engine to start smoking so you're forced to pull over while driving down the highway of life? Those people have to go if you want to start living your dream life. Stop the bus and kick them off. On the opposite end of the spectrum, those you trust the most are in the very front row of your bus, your most inner circle.

It's your bus, so you can get in the driver's seat and take control of your life. That starts by deciding who and who not. You also have to decide where everyone sits on the bus. The first row has the most access to your time, energy, and love. If they're in the first row, they are the most important to you and likely vice versa. The back row is for your fun friends, those who are fun to attend events with, but they're not the person you call when you're in crisis mode, and they're not the person you are most vulnerable with.

The middle seats are for those somewhere on the sliding scale between fun friend to trusted confidant.

All seats on your bus are special, coveted positions. It's important for you to remember that, or you'll leave the bus door open for anyone to get on. And that is not what we want to do.

One-Way Friendships vs. Mutually Beneficial Relationships

One-way friendships are the worst. You are pouring into this person, but it's not reciprocal. You eventually realize that you are supporting them, cheering for them, coaching them, and more, but they're not doing the same for you. It's absolutely draining to carry so much of this person's weight and not have any of your weight carried. That's when you wake up and realize this is a one-way friendship.

Mutually beneficial relationships are what you want, not the other way around. Friendships where you both walk away from brunch feeling happy, energized, and excited for the next time you hang out. You poured into them, and they poured right back into you. It was reciprocal, and you both feel it.

You're not keeping a tally of all interactions. This is more of a gut feeling and realization. But if you're looking for a sign, think about this: Are you always the one reaching out? If the answer is yes, just stop reaching out and see what happens from there.

Jealousy does not belong in your joy squad. I think we've all had that "friend," or shall I say faux friend, that always wanted what you have and was never happy with what they have.

What I know now is that they didn't value or recognize what they had for themselves and thus couldn't be satisfied. I have a natural joy, but not everyone does, and it's probably a good thing because for some, it's exhausting to be around me. This is why it's a beautiful thing that there are so many different types of people in the world, as we each bring a unique value. When you are comfortable and confident in your unique value, then there's no reason to be jealous.

Even in my darkest days of depression, I was still happy to learn of my friend's wins. I still cheered for them even when I couldn't cheer for myself. And the friends who are now my chosen family cheer for me even in their hardest days. I remember calling one of my girlfriends to tell her I'd gotten the largest contract in Goal and Grind's history. We were "scream happy" on the phone, and she was excited for me. Later in that call, she shared that she'd been laid off from her job. All I could think was that she just let me go on and on about my win and was genuinely excited for me, all the while she had the opposite going on for her. I wanted to know how to support her and what her needs were at this time.

Now imagine having someone in your joy squad who gets jealous of your wins, or who feels their losses prevent them from celebrating your wins. It's not healthy and will drag you down, minimizing your wins and eliminating space to celebrate them.

Using Discernment in Relationships

When people get on your bus, they're not automatically in the front or middle rows. It's perfectly fine to start them on the sidewalk, even.

Maybe they're newer in your life, and they have potential to move to the middle of the bus from the back of the bus; but you don't know yet because you're friend dating.

Honestly, this was a really hard lesson for me and continues to be. As an extrovert who believes the best in everyone, I have been burned and disappointed several times by letting people get to the middle of my bus too quickly.

We're having fun and enjoying each other's company. Then I realize we are not values aligned and that, in fact, something they value is harmful to me. There's a mourning period as I remember the good, not great, times that we've had together. However, I can't unsee or unknow what I've learned about them. If you've ever had a friendship end, you already understand this.

Keep in mind you can rearrange your joy squad anytime, especially as you evolve, because you might be growing in different directions. It's your bus, and you're in the driver's seat deciding who is on or off your bus of life.

Above all, remember that you don't have to be perfect, and you're growing. The person you were yesterday is not the person you are today, and the person you are today is not the person you're going to be tomorrow.

Walking Away and Letting Go of Misaligned People

It's okay. Just do it, you'll feel much better after releasing them. Before you know it, you'll be asking yourself how and why it took me so long to get to that.

I'm not perfect, I'll still let some Negative Nancys in, but I'll be quicker to walk away from them.

I learned how to do this at a young age, so it comes more easily because I've had a lot of practice; however, it's not lost on me that it can be very difficult.

Although painful, I am thankful because my decision to let go took me down a path of not accepting less than I am worthy of. I came to a realization that I have a choice in who I allow into my life, and now I like to think of it as "if you're not adding to my glow up," there might not be room in my life.

In the end, it's simple. I appreciate the people in my life, and I'm proud of the decisions I've made because they are my own. Every person in my life is special to me because I chose to have them in my life, to spend time with them, to grieve alongside them, to laugh with them, to cry with them, to celebrate successes with them, and, above all, to love them.

Whenever I'm trying to weigh whether or not someone still belongs in my life, I think to myself, does this relationship make me smile or does it make me frown? If it's a frown, then why am I entertaining it?

In each of your joy squads, there are moments to audit who is present (or needs to be) and build new connections, as well as to maintain existing relationships. In the next portion of this chapter, we will talk about each of the joy squads. In some, we'll dig deep into auditing, and in others, it might be building or maintaining. Keep in mind, regardless of whether we cover it for that specific joy squad, it is still relevant to it.

Your Personal Joy Squad

Let's inventory your personal joy squad. These are questions to help you with this activity:

1. Who is in your joy squad?

2. How do they bring you joy?

3. How do you bring them joy?

4. Do they subtract joy from you?

5. What's your values alignment?

6. Who is currently supporting your goals?

7. Who is draining your energy?

8. Who is boosting your energy?

These are the questions we're seeking to understand while auditing your personal joy squad.

It can be interesting as you might begin to gain a deeper appreciation for your nearest and dearest. It's also a tough exercise because, at times, you'll realize you need to restructure some of your friendships.

You'll know it's time to refresh a friendship based on how reciprocal you feel the relationship is, if you feel like you're forcing yourself to spend time with the person, or if you barely have common interests. Something to think about is whether you are always doing the outreach to them.

Someone once advised me that "You can't change the people around you, but you can change the people around you," meaning everyone has free will, and you cannot change that. However, you can change who you choose to give the privilege of being in your space.

Identify Gaps in Your Personal Joy Squad

What type of personal support is missing from your life? Return to your Conceptualization Chart that we made. Check out the personal column for your ten-year, five-year, and one-year goals. Then think about the type of support you'll need for those.

Maybe your goal is to meet your future husband and get married. If so, you might want to spend time with friends who are ready and willing to make introductions or consider hiring a matchmaker. Regardless of the situation, you are aiming to put yourself in a position to have this goal supported in a meaningful way.

Maybe you have a goal to start traveling internationally, but you've never done it before. Time to join a travel group! There's a whole world out there, and if you don't have anyone to explore it with, you could join a group travel trip that matches your interests and comfort level.

If you have a goal and you're missing someone to support it or to enjoy crushing it with, there are a plethora of groups out there, both online and in person. Do a quick search for what you're looking for, and I'm fairly certain you'll find options.

When you start building your personal joy squad, return to your Joy Bubble and seek out groups focused on its contents first. After you try something once, do a gut check to quickly move on from anything that doesn't serve you.

Maintain Your Personal Joy Squad

Let's start with the people who bring you joy, are aligned with your values, and support your goals.

Relationships take work, and the inputs of that work are the maintenance. Consider the following:

- When's the last time you told them you love them?

- When's the last time you told them you appreciate them?

- When's the last time you acknowledged all they do in your life?

- When's the last time you acknowledged how much they mean to you?

When I worked at my church, we read the book *365 Thank Yous: The Year a Simple Act of Daily Gratitude Changed My Life* by John Kralik. After that, we wrote thank-you notes at the beginning of every staff meeting. We might not have done one every day, but we wrote at least one a week. It was a beautiful practice that I actually need to reinstate. I'll never forget the day my pastor talked about the book from the pulpit. I remember him saying something to the effect of, "'Thank you' doesn't count if you never tell the person." That hit me hard because I'm great at writing to people, but I'm terrible at getting to the post office. So, my thank-you letters rarely get mailed.

In addition to gratitude, it's important to celebrate their wins, honor their birthdays (and their kids, too), check on them, and more. That's how you grow closer and remain in touch. Friendships take work, just like any relationship.

If you don't work on them, they'll fizzle. Just think about it: How can you be close to someone you don't interact with?

Your Professional Joy Squad = Your Personal Board of Directors

Your network is your net worth. People say that for a reason, and it's true!

We explored the concept of your personal board of directors in a previous chapter. This is essentially your professional joy squad, and it is the most structured of the joy squads. We also touched on building out your personal board of directors. I want to continue that topic here with how to maintain your personal board of directors.

Maintain Your Professional Joy Squad

Trust

Trust is a key component of maintaining your professional joy squad. My mother always told me that at the end of the day, all you have is your word. In corporate, I always respected the people who did what they said and said what they'd do. It was simple because many people have terrible follow-through. At work, everyone is a piece of a puzzle, and when one piece decides not to work with the others, everyone feels it: Everything is thrown off. Don't be the bent puzzle piece. It not only affects you and your team in the present, but it will also affect you later. You never know who is paying attention to your work ethic or who will be in a position to sponsor you in the future. No one sponsors someone they can't trust, because that reflects on them.

A great example of this is when Jenné Myers recommended me for my job at the aerospace company. We had lunch months after I started working there. She was so excited for me, and I thought it was just because I got the job (a job, finally!), but it was deeper than that. She said that my boss's boss (her friend) told her I was the best hand-off ever and that I was excelling at my job. She was beaming because she'd made the introduction, and that was a reflection of her just as much as it was of me, since she'd vouched for me. WOW! I didn't even know they talked that much, and I definitely didn't think they talked about me. But there it was, proof that if I got that job and performed poorly, there would have been a ripple effect on my career.

Touch Points

Maintaining your personal board of directors looks different, depending on the relationship, so I'll give you a few options.

Regularly scheduled touch points

There are people in your network who you'll want to establish regular points in time to connect with. It's always a good idea to ask someone how they would like to stay in touch. For every mentor I've had, I've asked this question, and then we agree on a cadence. Afterward, I email their assistant (with them cc'd) and ask for the meetings to be scheduled. For example, if we agree on meeting every other month, I'll send this note to their EA:

> Hi <insert EA's name>,
>
> Hope you're doing well. <u><insert mentor name></u> and I met today. I wanted to follow up to request your support in scheduling a bi-monthly virtual call with <u><insert mentor name></u>. Thank you for your support.
>
> Stay joyful!
> Bose

You can use this exact template! I know I have a million times. Just remember to always come to these conversations with clarity and ready to be specific.

I have a mentor, and I worked with her assistant to put bi-monthly times on the calendar for the two of us. When we meet, I come ready to:

1. Report out on progress (aka celebrations) because she wants to cheer for me.

2. Share what I'm struggling with so she can advise me, because that's why she's mentoring me.

3. Ask questions that she is uniquely positioned to advise me on. I know her job; therefore, I have an idea of what she can help with.

Each meeting is unique, as the report outs shared and asks are different. Every meeting supports my growth and feeds her desire to serve. If someone is mentoring you, they are not expecting you to ask about them, so it's a really refreshing thing when you do. They are expecting to pour into you, as that's what they've agreed to do.

There has been an instance where I asked my mentor how I could support her. Her response was to share my wins with her because she wants to know that what she's sharing with me is helping. From then on, I've been very intentional about giving her praise reports.

When you meet with someone for the first time, feel out their energy and alignment with your joy-driven goals. If it's a match, ask them at the end of the call if you can stay in touch. This is when you ask them (or suggest) a cadence for touching base.

As-needed touch points

There are people in your network that you know you can call on, but you don't necessarily have ongoing topics to discuss with them. It doesn't make sense to have regularly sched-uled meetings with them. Instead, reach out when you have a question or when you want to share something with them.

Unplanned encounters

There are people who you know aren't meant to be in your inner circle, and that's okay. Maintaining a professional connection with them can simply mean having a ten-minute conversation when you see them at an industry event. Maybe you like their content on LinkedIn or invite them to events that align with both of you. I'm always a fan of sending thank-you notes, as that's the bare minimum to keep a connection going with people in your outer circle. Basically, if you think about them, reach out, but if not, that's okay, too.

Your Health Joy Squad

Your health is your wealth. Take it seriously who is here to support this part of your journey, as it's the one that we often let fall by the wayside. As you audit your current health joy squad, here are some questions to ponder:

1. Does your current health team support your health goals?

2. What professionals are on your current health team?

3. What professional support do you need on your health team?

4. Who are the non-professionals who could support your health goals?

I can recall my first meeting with a member of my health joy squad, my internist. I sat there listening to her words in disbelief. My eating habits and non-existent physical workout routine were playing a part in my frequent migraines. I was in my twenties, eating whatever I wanted whenever I wanted, and never worked out. I didn't have anyone to work out with, and I also didn't know anything about working out. No one taught me how to lift weights, and I had never been to yoga before, so I didn't recognize the lingo. I definitely didn't know what a downward dog was. It was all foreign to me.

She explained to me that if I wanted to stop the series of prescription pain medications for my migraines, we could try editing my nutrition and adding exercise. She educated me on how my food choices were spiking my blood sugar, causing a yo-yo effect that resulted in migraines. My first time seeing an internist shifted my perspective. She focused on the root cause of the pain, whereas I had been treated for the symptom. After this encounter, I better understood my body and thus the type of physicians I needed in my health joy squad.

This is just my example, and each of our bodies is unique. At the core of this, keep in mind what your health goals are, as the people in your health joy squad will vary depending on your specific health-related goals. It's important to take into account that health philosophies differ widely. You will want to choose yours intentionally based on your needs.

Build Your Health Joy Squad

Start by getting real about your health philosophies. Go beyond your goals and into your beliefs about health. My health joy squad now includes my primary care doctor, therapist, women's health physician, optometrist, and dentist on the Western medicine side. (Due to a move, I am no longer able to have my internist, whom I mentioned earlier, as part of my health joy squad.) On the non-Western side, I have an Ayurvedic doctor who treats me and teaches me healing methods; I incorporate one new practice from him each year. There's also my acupuncturist, who seems like a magician. I can go in and tell her I'm feeling anxious, having knee pain from standing while leading a full-day workshop, or have a stress-related migraine, and she heals me.

Outside of medical professionals on your health joy squad, you might have a trainer at the gym, an adult sports league, instructors for the fitness classes you take, running groups, etc. The most important thing is to identify a form of physical activity that brings you joy. This is a very personal area where I don't suggest just going with the crowd.

Maintain Your Health Joy Squad

Flexibility helps with maintaining your health joy squad. Your body will change over the years. What serves you today is not always what served you yesterday, and also might not be what serves you in the future.

No matter who you are, when you experience a rapid change in your body, it feels weird. When your body changes, it is what it is, and you have to adjust, too. If you're of a certain age, you know what it's like to have to start wearing readers. It's sudden and uncontrollable. You need to read small-print menus at restaurants, but you can't without those pesky readers.

Having regularly scheduled appointments with the members of your health joy squad to discuss changes in your mind and body can offer you support through change. Talking to your accountability partners is also important, as you never know whether you might be going through similar challenges.

Your Financial Joy Squad

It's not uncommon to have never had anyone talk to you about money on a strategic level, beyond "Are the bills paid, or aren't they?" This was me, and I didn't know where to start, so I struggled and ended up with credit card debt, with zero clue how to pay it off.

Many people can support your financial journey, but that also depends on where you are. I started at rock bottom, so I'll take you on the journey I went on to get me where I am today: from being five figures in debt to having six-figure investment accounts. I'm not a financial advisor (which is why I have one), and everyone's journey is unique. So, this is just one example. Lean into your joy and create yours based on that. Spend according to your joy.

Creating a budget is a proactive plan for spending money before it's deposited in your account, rather than a reaction to what's left after you spend. Everyone creates their first budget at some point. It is helpful to get an accountability partner who is as serious as you are about getting financially organized, planning, and staying on track. Your accountability partner is someone with whom you feel very safe because you're talking about a very vulnerable and sensitive subject.

Talking about money can be triggering if you've ever had money trauma like me. That fear of opening mail and answering the credit card company's calls is so real. I paid off five figures of credit card debt, having my sorority sister, Lizzy, as my accountability partner while we took a financial planning course together. It literally changed the trajectory of my entire life, and is why I continue to be strict with my financial habits by having a pre-planned spending budget.

I shifted from reactionary spending that wasn't grounded in data or my goals to an informed, strategic budget built around my data and goals.

This is how the person or persons in your financial joy squad can affect your life (and your joy). They are essentially walking the path with you as they come to know your goals and support you with intentionality.

Maintain Your Financial Joy Squad

Establishing regular touchpoints with your financial joy squad is imperative for adjusting to your life changes.

As my life has changed, so have my financial goals. For example, the decision to go into full-time entrepreneurship meant that I needed a different level of support from my tax preparer, as I needed to add monthly bookkeeping to our relationship. It also meant my financial advisor would shift our strategies, since I'd no longer have a corporate 401(k) to contribute to and receive matching funds.

Maintaining my financial joy squad meant keeping them in the loop prior to changes, creating updated plans, and moving forward in financial sync with refreshed joy-based goals. It was tough as I was journeying into the unknown, but it would have been much tougher without my financial joy squad to support these endeavors.

My Finance Dream Team

I mapped out who all I needed on my finance joy squad and realized that not one person could do it all. I needed the following to support me with my financial goals:

1. **Financial advisor** – She handles all my investments. We have deep strategic conversations that start with where I'm at now, where I want to end up, and end with how we plan to get me there.

2. **Tax Preparer or Certified Public Accountant (CPA)** – She takes a strategic approach to understanding my employment, business, and investments to make tax strategy recommendations and then get my taxes done. If you do your taxes, you'll want to consider if you need this person. In my first job out of college, I was a contractor receiving a 1099. I didn't understand what that meant, and my taxes weren't prepared properly, so I got audited and ended up paying that bill off for the next decade. So, paying a few hundred dollars a year for someone else to do my taxes has been a priority for me since then because I was traumatized by taxes. The great thing is that I ended up saving money by having a tax preparer, as they're experts and knew about things I couldn't have known.

3. **Bookkeeper** – This one is for the business owners out there. She conducts my monthly analysis and

reconciles all accounts to ensure accurate reporting. Before I had my business, I actually did my own monthly bookkeeping of my personal financial records to make sure I was on target with my budget (spending categories, savings, etc.). It was a great temperature check for understanding progress.

4. **Banker** – Rather than simply engaging with a teller or the random customer service representative on the other side of an 800 number, having a relationship with my banker has been helpful in navigating particular needs as a business owner. I can call her anytime, and she will walk me through the account options.

Gentle reminder: This is who is on my finance dream team, as it aligns with my joy-rooted goals and my ability to execute them. Yours might look different, so don't go out and hire all these folks without first understanding what and who you actually need to adequately support your joy-driven financial goals. This is one of the main reasons I started this book with the Vision and Goals Method™: Everything that follows can be tailored to your needs.

As with the need to focus on a particular key area of life for your goals, there will be seasons when you shift your focus to a certain joy squad.

The key point to take away from this chapter is that, for each of the four key areas of life, you will have different types of support for those goals. As your goals shift, you'll want to consider whether you have the support you need by auditing your joy squad(s). Similarly, you might revisit this chapter when you need to think about cultivating new relationships in one of the four key areas. Additionally, this chapter is designed for when you need tools to acknowledge your joy squad and maintain healthy relationships with them.

JOY JUMPSTART

Acknowledge someone in your joy squad. Perhaps you write a thank-you note to a friend or family member. Consider calling someone and sharing what you appreciate about them. Or maybe send an email to the manager of someone who's been a great co-worker. Copy them on it so they can see you brag on them to their boss.

Letting those in your joy squad know how much you appreciate them is an important practice.

PART II

JOY THAT SUSTAINS YOU

JOURNEYS IN JOY:
FROM QUICKSAND TO CLARITY

Amy Clarice, founder of ClairvoyAgency, has this very special place in my heart because she's a total rock star. She's accomplished so much, and I'm really excited for you to read her story before we jump into the next section.

I'm inspired by all that she's done, and I know you will be, too. She truly embraced the Vision and Goals Method™ to understand and view her life holistically across the four key areas of life.

By late 2020, Amy Clarice had achieved the dream: published with Penguin Random House, built a nonprofit agency, and purchased a big house. She was at the height of her career. She was also drowning.

"I was like a boat at sea," she remembers. "We were sailing somewhere, but we didn't have a direction. I felt like we were treading water and weren't really bringing on new clients. Things were changing with a lot of our current clients because of their budgets."

A medical scare hit simultaneously. Clients pulled back. Revenue stalled. The heaviness was suffocating, not because life was hard, but because nothing made sense together.

Then came the reframe: Personal. Professional. Health. Financial.

Four separate categories. Four distinct truths demanding her attention.

Amy had never put a number on her health goals and never realized that, as a gay woman wanting motherhood, there was a ticking clock. Never connected that financial stability was the foundation for personal dreams.

"I felt like I was stuck in quicksand," she said. "It's like you can't figure out how to move from here to here, you know? You know you don't want to stay in this spot, but it just was difficult to figure out how do I get to the next level of what it is that I want to be doing?"

Does that sound familiar, friend? Well, the framework we're going to dig into soon was her way out.

First came financial clarity. She built a savings plan, divested from what didn't serve her, and reframed money from something that happened to her into something she could design. She sold the historic house that was draining her and moved into a home that aligned with her joy.

"Once I realized these are the things I need to get to the other areas of my life that bring me joy, why was I holding on?"

With money came honesty. Her business partner wasn't aligned with her vision of single motherhood. She restructured the partnership. She took a part-time development role at a non-profit, exactly what she needed. She learned to ask: What do I need? Who do I need?

In 2023, I read an email update from Amy. She shared, "One of my BIG main goals is coming true, and I really want to share with you." We got on the phone, at which point I was elated to learn of our first baby resulting from the Vision and Goals Method™.

Amy aligned her finances and career to make space for a baby. She had the clarity to openly share her goals, which led a friend to offer to be her sperm donor. Her darling son arrived in 2024, and their lives are full of adventure.

Amy took maternity leave, and today, she partners with aligned clients through her company, has savings, and radiates something she didn't have before: confidence.

"The feeling now is more confident in knowing that if I want something, I need to fully imagine it happening for me."

She didn't abandon her mission. She stopped carrying it alone.

CHAPTER 6

Create Alignment Across Your Whole Life

When I moved from Oklahoma City to Chicago with no job and no network, people thought I was crazy, but I knew I was living out a plan that was strategically aligned with my joy.

I had developed my life strategy (the same one we already discussed), and it was time to activate it!

Before uprooting my life, I had a 9-to-5 job and took on a second job on weekends, but I didn't change my spending habits. I saved all the extra money, gave six months' notice at my 9-to-5 office job, hired and trained my replacement, sold two-thirds of everything I owned, and moved to Chicago with a heart full of joy and clarity. It was a calculated risk, but people didn't understand that because they were used to living in fear of the unknown. Meanwhile, I embraced the unknown with curiosity and enthusiasm.

Everything about my life in Oklahoma was good, but I didn't love it. I wasn't on fire for my life. I was killing it in my professional life. But I was failing in my personal, health and even my financial lives.

I was only setting goals for my professional life. All the while, I felt unaligned, out of whack, and exhausted.

Then I began to see myself as a whole person. I wasn't just what I brought to the table at work, to someone else's table. I also had personal goals that deserved recognition. But, oh wait! I also had health and financial goals that needed to be recognized. That's when I started making goals in the four key areas of life (personal, professional, health, and financial), and I really started to see myself.

My goals were:

- Personal: Move to Chicago (my dream city).

- Professional: Transition to corporate philanthropy.

- Health: Build a workout routine.

- Financial: Create monetary stability.

This is how the Vision and Goals Method™ was born. I started to feel more balanced, began honoring myself, and excelling more at work. I created the Vision and

Goals Method™ when I found myself in a cycle of focusing solely on my professional life, without being intentional about the other key areas of life (personal, health, and finances).

When I developed this method, I was an Oklahoma City girl with big city dreams. Now I'm a Chicago woman who has dominated her goals in all four key areas of life...well, there's one personal goal I haven't hit, but I've shifted to focus on that personal goal more in 2026. Just as I've reminded you in this book, none of us is perfect, and there's room for flexibility within your goals.

I had always dreamed of living in a big city, but I didn't know how to make it happen. After all, I had a "great job" along with friends, family, and the stability of life where I lived. I didn't have the money to move, as every cost-of-living study said Chicago was way too expensive for me.

I found my ten-year anniversary of moving to Chicago journal entry and discovered how I reflected on all I'd accomplished as well as my own transformational growth. It was more than I imagined a decade prior: the people I built relationships with, the obstacles I overcame, and the career I'd engineered. I noted that I was living my dream job in my dream city, yet the dream had now expanded. I was ready for more calculated risks, dedicated focus, meaningful sacrifice, deep learning, and learning from my mistakes, as I knew those were the things that would grow me into my new dream-sized goals.

It's not about what is in my ten-year reflection. It's about you creating yours and being intentional about making space to look back at where you started and how far you've come.

And none of it would have been possible if I'd stayed in Oklahoma rather than pursuing my joy.

INTERCONNECTEDNESS OF THE FOUR KEY AREAS OF LIFE

The world has programmed us to separate and compartmentalize our lives, as though one aspect doesn't affect the others. The Vision and Goals Method™ focuses on the interconnectedness of the four key areas of life.

- Personal – Being strategic with your life

- Professional – Being productive with your career

- Health – Being consistent with your well-being

- Financial – Being intentional about your monetary resources

It can feel overwhelming. You see your ten-year vision, and it sounds great, but how do you get there? I want to set you up for success by taking you deeper into the Conceptualization Chart, where you set goals in the four key areas of life. Reference it often as a remembrance that progress is more important than perfection throughout your journey in joy.

Across the top are personal, professional, health, and financial. From top to bottom, it's ten-year, five-year, one-year. I encourage everyone to start at ten-year for two reasons.

First, because you already have your vision and it is included in your ten-year goals, start with those. Second, when you start at ten-year, you can break it down and say to yourself, "Five years from now is the halfway mark. Where do I want to be at the halfway mark if I'm really trying to arrive at a certain goal in ten years?" And then you have a clearer indication of what you need to work on right now, in this year. That keeps the one-year goals from feeling so overwhelming because you're no longer trying to reach the ten-year goals or a huge vision all at once.

You're trying to do that one small baby step that you can do this year that aligns with your vision that's rooted in your joy, rather than the world's expectations.

You might blur the lines of professional and financial, causing you to wonder what the difference is between the two. Your professional life is your career, and your financial life is your money. You can change career pathways or jobs, but still have the same money goals.

Additionally, you might be seeking clarification between personal and health. Consider this: Personally, you might want to travel or have a romantic partner, but your health is what you focus on with your doctors and your workouts to impact your physical being, etc.

PART III

Below are the examples for each of the four key areas:

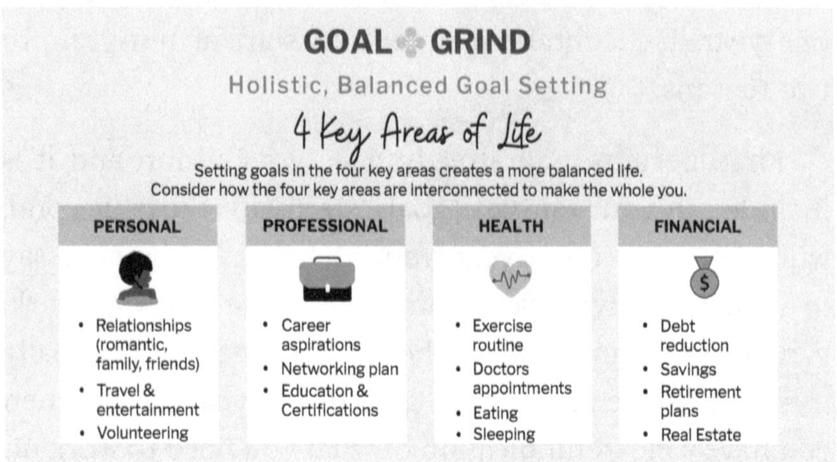

These examples are not an exhaustive list but rather ideas to help you begin thinking about your own.

This framework for understanding how the four key areas of your life are interconnected is so important because my client, Amy, never considered that having her house was killing her finances. Everyone always says, "Buy property," so she did it. But it was ruining her finances, so she sold the house and downsized, which is part of why she was able to afford her personal goal of getting pregnant on her own and becoming a single mother by choice.

This is why I don't believe in living a siloed life. We are whole humans, and until we look at ourselves holistically, no one else will either. Each area has a goal that needs support. Begin thinking of how you'll arrive at said goals, who's on your bus helping you achieve your goals, and the resources needed for you to complete said goals. Last, and equally important, you can begin thinking about how you celebrate achieving your goals.

The four key areas of life are not at odds with one another; they coexist harmoniously.

Each of the four key areas of life (personal, professional, health, and financial) is interconnected and has equal meaning in and for your life.

Think of it this way: When work is misaligned, it often leaks into finances through burnout, turnover, or stalled growth. When health suffers, it can affect the ability to focus at work, attributable to pain or brain fog. When financial worries become a constant, a scarcity mindset can impede the ability to dream of creative options due to fear or uncertainty. When personally unfulfilled, the sense of purpose can disappear, spilling over into a lack of motivation at work or in general.

The thing is, when you have your vision and your goals, you start to understand that it's okay to fully focus on one area in some seasons while you don't focus on the other areas as much. You know and understand that the other key areas have equally meaningful goals that you can (and will) pick up in another season.

For example, you might have a season where you are fully focused on climbing the corporate ladder. You're all in on your career so much so that you might be a little bit of

PART III

a crappy friend, mother, daughter, etc. In that time, you're not making it to all of little Deondre's basketball games. But then there are seasons where you couldn't care less about climbing the corporate ladder because you're fine staying in the same role, because it means you get to be fully focused somewhere else. Perhaps in this season you're now focused more on family time, so you are at all the basketball games. Or you have a health scare, surgery, or something makes you decide to buckle down on your health goals; therefore, other areas take a back seat. These are all great. The main thing is to make sure it's aligned with your joy, and to know your other goals, which serve as a tiny reminder in the back of your brain of how all your goals are connected. Additionally, this empowers you to communicate these with your joy squad so they can support you.

So, like for me, right now, everyone knows I'm in full-fledged writer mode. My phone is on DND all the time, and I'm in cafes or on my couch, writing day in and day out. I'm not at brunch. I'm not at the happy hour. I'm writing. My friends don't care because I've been upfront, honest, and most importantly, clear with them. They're actually so damn excited that they don't care that they're on the back burner in this phase of life. I'm comfortable with it as I understand how the book aligns with my other goals, so it's okay that all else is on the back burner during this time.

It can be hard, which is why we talked about having the right people in your joy squad who cheer for you even when you can't show up.

The first time I heard someone else talk about it this way was Thasunda Duckett when she was explaining her "diversified portfolio" approach to life. I was shocked and excited. She said there's no such thing as balance, and to look at your life like a financial portfolio, making sure it's diversified. The explanation was spot on with what I refer to as a balanced/holistic lifestyle, and I love it!

You start with your joy. Then you spread joy to those around you and work to sustain your own. It's interesting as these are not linear stages. There will be times when you're spreading joy, then you jump over to starting joy. It's also not a level playing field for each of the key areas of life. You might be spreading financial joy while you're starting your health joy, and that's okay.

When I moved the Chicago, I was trying to transition to a different career pathway that was new to me; therefore, I went back to start mode professionally. In my role in Oklahoma City, I was spreading joy as I'd mastered my role and was constantly working to support others by spreading joy as the welcome director at my church. Literally, I was hugging people, praying with people and connecting them to resources. My whole job was spreading joy. Even though my experience in Oklahoma City was valuable and would contribute later, once I got to Chicago, I was focused on transitioning careers, which took me back to start joy mode in my professional life. I was learning and trying new things to see what worked for me as I ventured into a new career pathway.

Your joy journey is so personally unique and intimate to you. It's similar to feelings in that no one can tell you it's right or wrong. It simply is how you feel. It's your joy; protect it and honor it.

In all stages of joy, you will experience learning, growth, and, unfortunately, sometimes shedding. Learn to invest in yourself as you level up. Grow into your rebirth. Shed people, places, and things that no longer serve you to make room for what does serve you.

Let's get into joy in each of the four key areas of life. In this chapter, we'll go through each one, while touching on how to start joy for yourself, sustain your joy, and spread joy to others.

Personal Goals

When you start talking about personal goals, you're talking about things like relationships (romantic, family, friends), travel and entertainment, volunteering, fashion, pets, etc. Personal joy isn't tied to your job, but it still deserves goals because you have desires and wants beyond work.

Personal joy is what you do in your free time, how you prefer to connect with your friends and family. Maybe you like to travel, go to comedy shows, volunteer, play sports, etc. It puts a giant smile on your face when you do it and makes you feel energized. If money were no object, what would you do with your time, where would you be, and who would be with you? Maybe you'd read a book, spend time traveling with your family, or maybe you'd be at a comedy show with friends or loving on your fur baby. Let's reinforce that this is not what you see on social media. Be introspective and consider how your body responds when you do these activities as well as your attention span for them. When you engage in activities you enjoy, you don't feel tired; instead, you want to keep going like you're binge-watching the latest season of *Bridgerton*, and when there's no more to watch, you check to see when Shonda is releasing the next season.

Making Time for You, Starting with Personal Joy

Going back to your Joy Bubble, use that as your foundation for life. Think about what is in your Joy Bubble and if you need to expand on it.

Start scheduling "me" time. Your me time is a time for you to recall the selfish energy we visited previously. I use the word *selfish* intentionally because, if you're anything like me, you need permission to stop helping, supporting, and doing things for others. Take time to sit in stillness with yourself. Treat yourself like you'd treat your best friend. Give yourself that level of care, thought, and attention.

Personal joy is one of the hardest to sustain because of FOMO. Get so clear on your own joy that you spend a lot of time saying no to what doesn't serve you in order to be able to say yes to what does serve you. Social media will tempt you with perfectly photoshopped imagery of events, concerts, etc., that are designed to make you want to spend money on them.

During the course of writing this book when I opened social media and saw my friends at events, the thought didn't cross my mind of "wish I was there" because if I had wanted to be there, I would have been, but in the moment, I was writing (they knew it, and I knew it). It's that simple. It took a lot of practice, learned discipline, and reminding myself to focus on my joy to get here. I'm not perfect at the no FOMO life, as there are times I see an ad and buy. You are human. Give yourself grace that this will happen.

Everyone talks about setting boundaries, but no one talks about how to implement them. I'm a strategic thinker, so I literally look at my activities and consider what brings me joy. If it doesn't, I no longer do it. Period! In addition to not doing said activity, I am clear with my friends. A great motivator for this is your financial goals. If you're saving to buy a house, for example, use that goal to motivate you to reduce spending in other areas.

To sustain your personal joy, it helps to be surrounded by people who are confident in their joy so much that they don't need you to participate in every activity they do. They support your joy even when it's not for them.

Sharing your goals with your nearest and dearest will help you remain accountable to yourself because they'll be so excited to see you win! They'll ask you how things are going and what they can do to support you. If not, it might be time to shed some folks to make room for those who cheer for you.

A brief reminder from chapter 5: You can't change the people around you, but you can change the people around you.

Professional Joy

I think the saying goes, "Enjoy what you do, and you'll never feel like you work a day in your life." Some would say there can't be joy in work. I'd like to challenge that, not only because I, as well as others, am living proof that you can, in fact, enjoy your work, job, or profession, but because there is proven research that it's actually helpful to enjoy the work you do. I do understand it's not always common to be in a role you enjoy; however, let's talk about ways to shift that for you.

Your Journey to Start Professional Joy

It starts with understanding your unique purpose and value add. Adding value to your team and work offers a certain level of satisfaction to your soul.

Purpose is the overlap between what brings you joy and what your talents/skillsets are. We've talked about how finding your purpose is the foundation for position-ing yourself professionally to build your reputation in something you're good at that also brings you joy. Now we'll talk about how having a role with your purpose amplifies your professional joy.

Often, people refer to jobs with purpose as those in the social impact space or the nonprofit sector. While those are great roles, that is not what I mean by "purpose" here. I like to clarify that the definition of purpose within this text is the crossover between your joy factors and your income-generating skills—it is unique to the individual.

You deserve a career that brings you fulfillment. Yes, it's nice to get a paycheck, but what's equally fabulous is to really enjoy the work you do. This can be a difficult mindset shift, as our entire lives, the story we've been told is that work is something to get done, something we have to do, rather than something we get to do and can enjoy.

I'm not referencing opportunity as the moment when your boss comes to you with an "opportunity" in which they'll dump more on you without compensation or recognition. I'm talking about getting to do what sets your heart on fire! The job you're both part excited and part curious about. I want you to grow and glow in your next opportunity. Imagine having a job that moves with you and ages with you like a fine wine.

The next time someone says, "Everyone wants this job. You should be grateful for it." you'll be able to pause and consider your joy rather than what everyone else wants. You won't just say yes to everything that comes your way (even if that means staying in your current role). You'll be able to clearly ask yourself what makes sense for you and then choose that.

If you're having trouble figuring out whether you have professional joy, keep it simple. Consider whether the job at this place makes you smile or frown. Does it energize you or drain you? When you get home from work each day, are you counting down the days, hours, and minutes until the weekend? Are you excited and chatting about this job nonstop? Your answers to all these questions affect your energy, which is a telltale sign of your joy factors.

Professional joy is one of the hardest to protect because you're constantly subjected to change, and with change always comes norming, storming, and forming (the cycles of change). There are changes in people, policies, and structure, as well as so many other potential changes to navigate. The important thing is for you to remain constant in what you do and why you do it (for yourself...not them).

That's how you protect your energy. Be your own north star. Fully understanding your boundaries and your goals will enable you to make joy-based decisions when changes occur. If you've ever been in corporate, you've likely heard the phrase "expect the unexpected" because there are a number of different types of changes that happen, anything from leadership to technology to strategies and priorities. It's all subject to change (sometimes with what feels like zero notice).

PART III

Sustaining your professional joy means knowing you can walk away when, and if, you need to. Hint, hint: this ties into the importance of seeing the connection between your financial goals and professional goals.

> *You won't be ready for the main stage until you've spent time backstage*
>
> —Bose Akadiri

There will be times when you're so eager to move to the next stage in your career. You know what it is and you can name it so clearly, but you just can't seem to get that job. This is when it's important to remember that everything you do today is building toward your tomorrow. Take the current role as your learning experiment, preparing you for your big, beautiful future.

You can find meaning in your role, even as you build toward a larger vision for yourself. You can appreciate your role for where it's taking you tomorrow and for what you're learning. And speaking of learning, you are not letting life come towards you. You are consistently going out and grabbing opportunities that align with your future self. You can find opportunities to advance yourself by:

- Reaching out to leaders in the department you want to be in to learn from them, connect with them, and showcase your drive.

- Strategically taking on stretch assignments that position you for growth and visibility. Beware of stretch assignments that do not align with your joy-rooted goals, as they can become deterrent distractions.

- Sending thank-you notes to people you have coffee chats with, further enabling them to remember you.

- Scanning all company benefits and using the ones that serve you. For example, there might be education benefits or sabbatical options.

- Staying away from and not getting wrapped up in office drama as it never serves you; it only distracts and potentially places you in an untoward light.

This is when you're in your zone! No one can snatch that away from you. This is when joy is both your offense and defense in the office.

Health Joy and Goals

When you start talking about health goals, consider what resonates from a perspective of triggering pleasure rather than pain. Keep in mind the pleasure is not always immediate; however, the pain typically is. These are all deeply unique to each person, so I want to start by acknowledging that this is not a one-size-fits-all. It's a framework that will help you find what size fits you.

Examples of health joy are vast, but here are a few to get your brain going: exercise routines, doctors' appointments, nutrition habits that align with your body, sleep hygiene, supplements, spa time, etc.

Get curious about your body, both mentally and physically. This is not the time to compare yourself to others. Just remember, your only competition is who you were yesterday because the actual goal is to help her improve, which is why she's the barometer and not anyone else.

Within our health, there's a mind-body connection. Physical health is more than just working out. It's also your sleep and eating habits.

I am a huge fan of Ayurvedic medicine, which is a 5,000+-year-old science from Kerala, India that heals via three components:

1. What you put in your body.

2. What you put on your body.

3. How you move your body.

I see my Ayurvedic doctor once a year, and it does wonders for my mental and physical health. I've come to understand it as a compliment to what my Western medical doctors prescribe.

This is what works for me and has evolved over time as I've learned more. This is not a prescription, as I am not a doctor, but rather a spark to remind you to listen to your own body and explore what does work for you.

If you're unsure what resonates with your body, consider what energizes you versus what drains you.

Is there a form of movement that when you're done, you can feel a glow from the inside out, and you have a giant smile on your face? If you've experienced that, that's your thing. If you haven't experienced it, maybe consider some good old-fashioned trial and error exploration.

Finding your physical health jam can start by exploring different types of movement. Focus on finding ones that feel fun for you...rather than ones that feel like torture. Gone are the days of saying "no pain, no gain." I'm not sure where that came from, but it's not true. You deserve to enjoy what you're doing. Can it be tough and even challenging? Yes, heck yes, it's going to be challenging at times, but at no point does it need to be painful.

Most fitness studios now offer free trials or discounted first-week classes. Try those and pay attention to how you feel while you're there. Think about whether you felt comfortable and welcome in the space because that's how you know it's nurturing for you. If it's a space you'd feel excited to return to, that signals you might enjoy engaging in this activity again. You'll want to notice whether you felt stretched and/or challenged, with motivation to go further, but without risking pain. Maybe you learned something new about your body or the science of the human body that intrigued you, possibly even gave you a lightbulb moment. These are signals to look for to know if it's right for you. And not just if the particular workout is right for you, but also if the particular gym or fitness studio could be your jam.

My mom and I have found some overlap that allows us to go together and support each other's health joy, but we are not the same in our movement joy. So, one of the most important things to take note of when you're trying out activities is whether they meet you where you're at on your journey and have the potential to grow with you over time.

Have grace and understanding with yourself and be realistic. It's wild to think you can go from no movement to running a marathon. Not only is it wild, but it can also be dangerous to your physical health.

One of my best friends is a marathon runner who consistently runs a 6:28-minute mile the entire marathon. It's so incredible I cried the first time I saw her run. I cried because of the look of pure joy on her face during that marathon. She enjoys being outside, seeing the city, and accepting the beers people hand her along the route.

The thing is, she doesn't just wake up and run a marathon. She trains for it basically year-round. The training varies depending on the season and the timeline, but there's a consistent plan to get her across the finish line. She's the personification of the saying, "it's not a sprint; it's a marathon." When I think of setting and crushing goals, I don't have a microwave version of my methodology to offer you. It's more like a Dutch oven which simmers over time to produce a well-crafted meal.

Things that can help you start health joy are:

- Listening to your body

- Finding habits that feel like self-love rather than self-punishment

- Focusing on preventative maintenance

- Understanding the root cause of illnesses

Take these into account to create your own rituals that excite you and motivate you to engage in them daily!

Now that you've learned your body's signals, you can be more intentional about listening to them and honoring them. You want to get so in tune with your body's whisper signals that you are able to redirect before the whispers become screams of desperation. How do I know? Oh, I've been there before!

I had to take a full stop break from life because I hadn't been listening to the signals. Then, I was diagnosed with depression and high anxiety. When I really think about it, they don't ever really go away; it's like you just learn to live with them. That's why now I am even more careful with my mental and physical health to ensure I don't get back to that breaking point again. It wasn't fun, but it was necessary for my breakthrough.

Create a routine for yourself. For example, I learned what I need to maintain my mental and physical health, so I created a loose schedule that aligns with my budget. It looks like this:

Daily	Weekly	Monthly	Quarterly	Annually
Stretching Ayurvedic supplements Three meals Chinese herbal tincture	Running Yoga, pilates, or barre3 Journaling Therapy	Massage to refresh muscles from workouts Acupuncture	Evaluate what's working and what's not working, and make adjustments Teeth cleaning (bi-annual)	Ayurvedic Panchakarma Well woman exam Vision exam

The shocking thing is, I can feel it in my bones when I stop my routine. The more you try what works for your body, the more you'll be able to create your own bespoke routine. Keep in mind, you don't have to do it all every day. There will be things that you do only once a year, and they sustain you for the year, or even health items that you do only once in a lifetime.

Spreading health joy can be as simple as being someone's accountability partner and/or modeling healthy habits. The most important part is providing judgment-free support. A great example of this is running groups. When I joined Black Girls Run, I was in maybe the best shape of my life. Twice a week, I had a fun-filled run with ladies in my neighborhood. We laughed, we had real talk, and we ran. The running group brought us together, but the accountability and joy kept us together. They modeled healthy behaviors for me in a way I hadn't seen before. These women also created a judgment-free space. Some were multi-marathon runners, some were just starting their running journey, and some were in between. It didn't matter where you were on your journey; there was a spot for you. I'd been a solo runner for a long time and finally understood why people loved running groups.

Last and most importantly, spreading health joy means that you're normalizing taking breaks. When I think about sharing and supporting others in their health journey, I can't help but think about my marathon bestie again. She just really enjoys marathon running, and she's also very serious about downtime and recovery. I learned from her how to show myself grace and to incorporate intentional recovery, which I appreciate so much.

Financial Goals

When you start talking about financial goals, you're talking about things like debt reduction, savings, retirement plans, real estate, etc.

I'll be honest and share that this is probably the hardest area to accomplish joy in. It's hard because it's complex and can be riddled with emotional trauma, coupled with deep misconceptions and embarrassment.

Joy in Money

We've been programmed not to seek joy in money. I don't believe that at all. It's taboo to ask for more at the workplace because you "should" be humble and appreciate what you have. I don't agree with this because you can both appreciate what you have and aspire to gain more. It's okay to find joy in financial freedom; they call it freedom for a reason.

During this part, I encourage you to confront where you are with money. There are phases to your money journey. We'll talk about those, but keep in mind, I'm not a financial advisor...and neither are those kids on TikTok. I can't tell you how much I encourage you to get yourself a certified financial advisor you can be vulnerable with—vulnerable enough to share your dreams as well as your scary bits with. One who you trust to be honest with you and who has the smarts to advise you toward wealth beyond your wildest imagination. Every time you leave your financial advisor's office, you should feel smarter.

The Joy of Money!

That's right. I said it. The joy of money, and specifically talking about it, not just spending it. I believe...and more than believing, I know that there can be joy involving money. For those of us who didn't grow up with an abundance of money, we learned to be humble, or even worse, we learned that being humble and not yearning for money was an admirable trait.

You can free yourself from the chains and educate yourself toward financial joy or, as some like to call it, freedom. Here's the thing: Money doesn't lie! Because 1 + 1 will always equal 2. There's no room for errors or elaborations because money doesn't lie.

When I started setting goals for my personal life, goals for my health, and goals for my career, they all came back to money. How can you achieve personal goals like travel, shopping, gifts, moving, donating to nonprofit organizations, and more? Whatever it is, it's going to take money to get there.

Financial joy starts with knowing your joy. Once you know your joy, you can make strategic financial decisions that align with it.

Getting a financial accountability partner saved my life. As a single woman, it can feel incredibly lonely and isolating to try to do it all on your own. My church in Oklahoma City offered a finance class as part of its Wednesday night Bible study program. I had no idea what to expect, but it truly shaped my fundamental understanding of personal finance, which I still apply today. We watched training videos, followed along with our workbooks, and most importantly, paired up with an accountability partner. This was a course my sorority sister and I took together. We paired up...and...well...bared our financial souls to each other.

It was scary. It was empowering. It was so necessary.

I had never talked about money so vulnerably and openly. It was like being naked and baring it all because we faced the reality of our financial state of affairs, but that gives you such a deep understanding of your money and equips you to make shifts in your finances or other areas of your life to support your financial goals. It also releases you from isolation as you realize you're not the only person in a similar position.

Doing that class with my sorority sister as my accountability partner, I paid off five figures of credit card debt and started my Chicago savings plan. It meant I moved to Chicago without credit card debt, which was huge for me. I sacrificed going out to dinner with friends and opted to cook and eat at home so I could save money. During that time, I also stopped spending money on charity fundraisers because I needed to pour into my own cup before I could pour into others'.

It took discipline. It took sacrifice. But above all, it took knowing my joy. Not a single sacrifice ever felt like one because I had a deep understanding of what the gain would be. The gain was me moving without the shackles of credit card debt, having financial peace, and building a foundation of freedom because needing someone else's money sure doesn't feel free.

Connect your Joy Bubble to your financial goals and let it guide you in setting your budget. Having joy in your finances is about blocking out the noise and refusing to keep up with the Joneses because your joy might not be theirs, and that is perfectly fine.

This became crystal clear when I was planning my move to Chicago. My joys included international travel and living in a walkable city; however, general cost-of-living studies didn't account for my joy factors. I needed to do my own cost-of-living math based on my joy.

When I subtracted all the expenses associated with having a car, I realized that I could put those funds toward a higher rent and pretty much break even. That meant my less expensive OKC rent, combined with car expenses, was equivalent to my new Chicago rent. This aligned with my joys.

Spreading financial joy requires empathy and remembering who you were when you knew nothing about your finances (if that was ever you). You need the ability to share your financial gems without judgment. Not all of us grew up with parents who had a financial advisor on speed dial. I know I didn't, so when it was time to learn it was scary and I didn't know where to turn.

I am beyond grateful to my friends who spent hours upon hours talking to me about everything from what meetings with their financial advisors covered to what they needed to do after the meetings to ensure the plan was executed successfully.

Spreading financial joy also means meeting people where they are. There are phases to one's financial journey, and some of us had to start in the negative...seriously. Not everyone even starts at zero.

The phases are:

1. **Budgeting** – By budgeting, I mean planning (not reacting). It's not enough to just know you don't overdraft your account each month; you need a plan for your money, or it will make one for you. You'll want to sit down and put the money into budget categories before you spend it. That will cultivate the habit of proactive planning rather than reactive responding. It will prompt your brain to consider whether an expense aligns with your joy before making it. Using the future homeowner example, when you get a sale email alert rather than thinking, "I'll save money by buying (insert name of item you had zero plans of purchasing prior to said email)," you'll think to yourself, "Spending $500 on this will put me behind in my down payment savings goal." I want to take a moment to recognize that there might be times when you create your budget and realize you're in a deficit (expenses outweigh your income). You're not alone. I've been there and so have countless others. If this is your experience, try not to feel overwhelmed or discouraged; focus on what you can control and work on it.

2. **Saving and/or debt reduction** – After you fully understand your budget and are consistent with it, then you start saving money and or paying off debt. Debt repayments are part of the budget, and once the debts are paid off, you can shift those funds into the savings category. It's wise to build in rewards for yourself at each milestone. So maybe, for each credit card you pay off, you treat yourself with the next monthly payment you would have had to make on that card. Then you proceed to apply that monthly payment toward paying off another card or toward savings if you've paid off all cards.

3. **Investing** – After you're feeling really good about your budget and having your debt paid off and an emergency fund, it's time to start investing outside of your company retirement plans. If you're like me, this phase can feel weird. You have money left over each month, and it's going toward something you can't see, touch, or feel. It's being invested in your future.

4. **Wealth building** – I think there's more after investing, but guess what. I'm not there yet, so I'm excited for someone to meet me where I'm at and be a joy spreader to me in these next phases.

Your money moves look very different at each phase, so if you're talking to someone like they're in wealth-building mode, but in reality, they're learning to budget, it's like you're speaking another language.

Meeting someone where they're at is a beautiful thing when it comes to finances because it unlocks opportunities like you've never seen before. Keep in mind that when you meet someone where they're at, you're supporting their goals (not your goals for them!).

And as with all the other four key areas of life, one of the most powerful ways to spread financial joy is to model it. Admittedly, this one is a little trickier because talking about money can be triggering.

I've found that the more joy I have in finances, the more comfortable I am talking about it. I've essentially normalized talking about budgeting and saying no to things that don't bring me joy, as they have no business being in my joy-driven budget. I'm not embarrassed to say, "Oh that's out of the budget" when it comes to an event ticket or a restaurant that I won't be going to. You might not relate to my exact experience, but you know the feeling of wanting to say no to something, yet feeling pressure to say yes.

JOY JUMPSTART

Get your Conceptualization Chart out and pick one area of life to focus on for the next thirty days.

Read through the full list to help you determine which area is most pressing and needs your attention now.

Take one goal from the one-year box to work toward these next thirty days.

PART III

CHAPTER 7

Align Your Team With Purpose

It doesn't feel good to be isolated while working on a team. You might be a lone wolf in the day-to-day of getting work done but at the end of the day it is a wonderful feeling to see how your work fits in with the overarching team's work as well as the broader organization-wide goals. This is one of the reasons I was quickly taught to attend the quarterly earnings calls of the companies I worked for. I might not be super financially savvy or be able to understand the full scope of the calls, but they gave me a good idea of what was important to the company and what wasn't a top priority.

PURPOSE DRIVEN LEADERSHIP METHOD

The Purpose Driven Leadership Method is all about creating a triple win. By triple win, I mean a win for you, your team, and your organization.

I can't fully take credit for the triple win concept, as my first boss at the global aerospace company gave it to me. She was constantly focused not only on her wins but also on how our team's wins supported the company's broader goals. This stuck with me as it creates alignment not only from top down but more so from the bottom up. This is how I learned to build strategies in which we'd all shine, and that would also be understood cross-functionally. When you start a project with this in mind, it supports your future work of communicating the project's outcomes, especially if the project results in changes outside of your team. People can understand better when there's a throughline connecting them to the team and the team to the broader company.

As we move through the steps of the Purpose Driven Leadership Method, keep in mind your audience as a leader. It's more than simply your team or your boss. It's your boss's boss, your peers on other teams, and oftentimes even external stakeholders. You can't make everyone happy, but consider an outcome where everyone can appreciate at least one part of the puzzle as it positively affects their work.

Step 1: Recall the Joy of Leadership

Return to a time when you longed to be a leader. What was it that made you want to be a people leader rather than an individual contributor?

The first step in being a purpose-driven leader is to tap into the joy that brought you to this point in your career.

Maybe you loved the work and wanted to support others in doing this work. Or maybe you had a leader from whom you learned how not to lead, and now is your chance to do things differently with the team. It might have even been the promise of a raise. It could be neither of these, and that's okay, too; however, there was something that made you raise your hand and step into the role of leading this team.

I want to pause for a moment and acknowledge again that our joy can change. If this exercise leads you to realize that being a people leader no longer brings you joy, that is okay. It's more than okay; this is your first step in exploring your next best move.

In the meantime, keep building your Joy Bubble, and this time, build it through a lens of what about leading this team, your team, brings you joy.

Step 2: Validate Team History

Now that you are centered on your own joy, specifically related to leading your team, we can move on to the next step of examining the current state of your team.

Your team has made great strides, and they (as well as you) deserve to be recognized for them. Rather than starting from scratch, put yourself in a position to build upon a solid foundation.

SWOT Analysis

It's not just a SWOT analysis. It is putting yourself in a mindset of "My team is already great."

Conducting a thorough SWOT analysis each year can uncover a lot about your team. Just as you might easily forget to highlight your own wins, it's easy to forget to recognize your team's wins. Think of the SWOT analysis as a 360-degree view, taking into account the good, bad, and everything in between, positioning the team to build from facts.

◄---------------- Positive ---------------------------------- Negative ----------------►

Strengths	Weaknesses
• Internal factors that are positive	• Internal factors that are negative
Opportunities	**Threats**
• External factors that are positive	• External factors that are negative

(Left axis: Internal Factors / External Factors)

PART III

Often, we don't spend enough time really considering the subtle differences between strengths and opportunities, or between weaknesses and threats. Strengths and weaknesses are within your team's control as they are characteristics of the team. Opportunities and threats are beyond the team's control, as they are external factors that will occur regardless of the team's actions. The additional consideration with opportunities and threats is that you might not know what they are at the time of the SWOT analysis, as the world is ever-evolving and rapidly changing.

I recommend starting with what is within the team's control, then moving to what is not.

Strengths are the team's positive attributes. Collectively, what are you great at? Are there advantages that the team has? What differentiators set your team apart from others? Examples of strengths are strong cross-functional collaboration, deep subject-matter expertise, adaptable during change initiatives, and consistently meets deadlines and KPIs.

Weaknesses are the team's negative attributes. Collectively, what do you struggle with? Are there knowledge gaps or challenges within the team? What does the team need to improve, or where does it need additional support? Examples of weaknesses include communication silos between sub-teams, slow decision cycles, skill gaps in emerging tools/technologies, or reactive rather than proactive planning.

Opportunities are external factors that positively affect the team. Consider external trends or market needs that your team can leverage to their advantage. Are there emerging trends you can capitalize on, or a new technology you can leverage in the team's work? Examples of opportunities include market gaps, technological advances, and upward economic shifts.

Threats are external factors that could have a negative effect on the team. Think about risks that are outside of your control. Are there any obstacles that might hold your team back? Have you seen any negative factors outside your control that affect your entire industry? Examples of threats are budget cuts or hiring freezes, regulatory or compliance changes, competing teams gaining internal influence, and loss of a major client or account.

All teams have items in each quadrant of the SWOT analysis boxes. The real question is how you identify these, as well as leverage them to propel the team and increase forward momentum.

Identifying items in each quadrant takes time. It's a practice you can start on your own, but ultimately, you will want to set aside time each year for the team to do together. Depending on the size and structure of your company, you can start this exercise at the executive level and then perform it separately at the department level. Because the sales and marketing teams have different KPIs and purposes within an organization, you should conduct separate SWOT analyses. Think of it this way: These are the exercises to do at the annual offsite, so you conduct them

PART III

based on the team that would be at said offsite. An example would be that at the executive level, you recognize a weakness in the form of marketing, which is broad; whereas, at the level of the marketing team, you would be more granular, breaking down why that weakness exists, and it might be something such as the marketing team being stretched thin from having too large a workload.

When you perform a proper SWOT analysis, you can begin to see a lot of areas that you can all take advantage of. For example, if one of the team's strengths is excellent client relationships, then you can use that to your advantage when describing deals. On the other hand, if you know that one of your team's weaknesses is inconsistency, then you can work toward building systems to support the creation of consistent practices across the team.

Let's see the SWOT analysis in action. For example, a leadership team gathers for its annual off-site to reflect on the past year and set priorities for the year ahead. One of the key discussions centers on improving how the organization launches new strategic initiatives. The team decides to conduct a brief SWOT analysis to guide their planning.

← ---------------- Positive ------------------------------------- Negative ----------------- →

	Strengths	**Weaknesses**
Internal Factors	• strong leadership bench with track record of delivering large initiatives • positive cross-functional collaboration • informed decisions by leadership that are based on company's solid internal data • innovative team members	• struggles in the early stages of initiatives • lack of clearly defined priorities, pulling teams in different directions and causing stress and overwhelm • breakdowns in intradepartmental communication during planning phases • confusion about ownership and timelines stems from communication challenges
	Opportunities*	**Threats**
External Factors	• improve alignment establishing clearer decision-making frameworks • define priorities earlier in the planning cycle investing in stronger project management processes • implement cross-department communication tools to help teams better move from idea to execution • formalize how lessons learned from past initiatives are captured, documented, and applied to future efforts	• slower execution • frustration among employees who are eager to move forward but lack clarity • competitors gain an advantage in the marketplace because they are able to mobilize more quickly around new opportunities • erosion of confidence in leadership's ability to translate strategy into action when there are repeated in efficiencies

*These are not examples of opportunities, but are examples of actions the team might take in light of the opportunities it discovered.

PART III

The SWOT discussion gives leaders a structured way to acknowledge what is working well, address internal gaps, mitigate potential external barriers, and identify practical steps that position the organization for stronger performance in the coming year.

Team Accomplishments

The other part of validating your team's history is to honor the accomplishments by naming them. It is helpful to have processes in place to do this throughout the year and then aggregate it by quarter at the end of the year. You can always add to it at the end of the year, but it is much easier if you make time regularly to build this list. Similar to regularly recognizing your own accomplishments, leaders rooted in joy and moving with purpose recognize their team's strides.

At year's end, you'll want to look at the team's great work and accomplishments by quarter, as this will help you in setting goals as well as understanding trends and peak times.

This is also an exercise you can start on your own, then work through with the team. If you're doing this regularly with the team, it might look like a bi-weekly deadline to submit your wins tied to current projects and KPIs. Assign a point person, maybe your EA or chief of staff, to collect and aggregate these so that you can present them at your monthly team meetings. It's a great way to incorporate routine recognition throughout your team, no matter the size. Provide instructions for everyone to share major project milestones, product launches, and team changes (hirings, promotions, or departures). Also consider any awards or certifications the team receives collectively, as well as those given to individuals.

Sharing at team meetings isn't the only way to report these to your team. You might have an internal newsletter or regularly use a collaborative workspace (Teams or Slack, etc.). You'll want to decide on the format for sharing and what to share where. For example, project milestones may be presented in team meetings along with a brief update, while awards are shared in the team's collaborative workspace. You'll have to do it in alignment with your team's culture, but the most important part is that it gets done.

Step 3: Revitalize Team Strategy

Having an understanding of the team's SWOT and accomplishments broken down by quarter, you are now ready to review the team's mission statement and strategic objectives to determine whether they still align with the team's work.

If your team has never created a mission statement, that's okay. This is the perfect opportunity to make one. The bonus is that you can use my mission statement formula.

This doesn't need to be neat and perfect to start with. Just focus on getting your thoughts out; then you can truncate and fine-tune them. Just think, if the idea was never thrown out in the drafting phase, you wouldn't be able to consider it in the final version.

PART III

Your Team Mission Statement

A key indicator of team alignment is when you can ask any member of the team about the team and hear a similar variation of the same statement. Everyone knows the mission. Everyone knows the goals. Everyone can speak to them confidently. There's a collective understanding. Let's visit the components of a mission statement.

Purpose: Why does the team exist?

Action: How do we fulfill our purpose?

Impact: Who do we serve, and how will they be better because of us?

Values: What principles guide how we work together?

Aspirations: Where are we headed, and what's the future vision?

After you brainstorm each of these, you'll begin to see trends that will help you narrow down the parts you'll use to construct the team's mission statement. Work with your team to brainstorm and fine-tune this so that they see themselves reflected in it. If you are a leader at a smaller company, you might be able to do this all together; however, if you're at a larger organization, you'll want to do this with the leadership team, then share it with the broader group for feedback prior to finalizing.

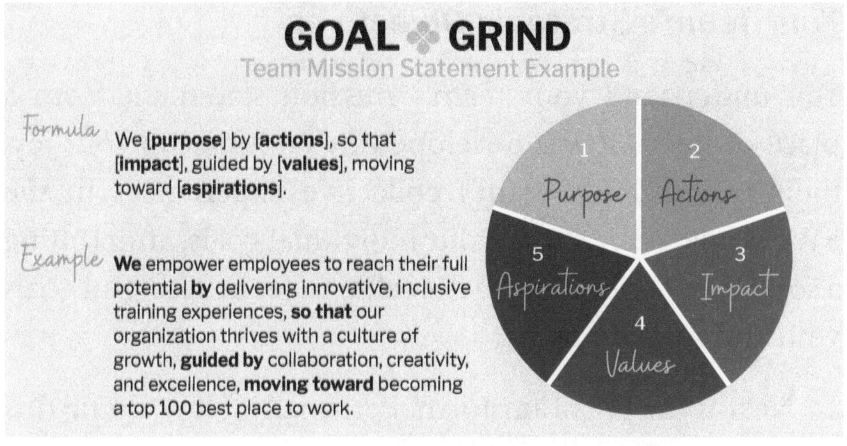

While you're working on this, say it out loud to your-self (and others). Reading it silently will always feel different than saying it out loud, as you'll begin to notice sticky points. You'll also be able to see if you could say it to someone off the cuff to describe your team. Think of this like your team (or organization's) elevator pitch. We've moved from individual community building and networking toward doing this as a team. When moving as a team, consistency is key, so make sure your mission statement gives everyone on the team an opportunity to weigh in. That's probably the hardest part and why off-sites can be such a valuable time for teams.

After you have your mission statement solidified, take a break. High-five a co-worker. Maybe even do a sigh of relief. They might look like just a few words strung together, but they are much more and take a lot of mental brain power to construct. This is an accomplishment you can celebrate as a team and individually.

Your Team's Strategic Objectives

You understand your team's mission statement from a place of joy as it was developed by considering your joy, their joy, and the team's collective experiences in the SWOT analysis. As with your individual goals, after setting a solid foundation, you're now able to set meaningful goals with and for your team.

Next is the big brainstorm. Personally, I love doing this on a giant whiteboard. It's not one hundred percent necessary for getting it done, but it can be helpful to visual learners on your team. Print the team's list of accomplishments as well as the SWOT analysis so that they're both fresh in everyone's minds. At the top of the whiteboard, write down the team's mission statement. After that, ask everyone to scribble down everything they want to get done this year—big, small, and in-between. This is how you'll identify the team's goals for the upcoming year. You could have them use dry-erase markers to put it on the whiteboard or you could use sticky notes that they then place on the whiteboard. I prefer sticky notes as they're useful for our next step.

Maybe they want to create a new system to streamline cross-department communication or implement a process for prioritizing initiatives. It is all valid. It can also be helpful to have a few pre-filled sticky notes on the board to help get everyone's creative engines flowing. As people are writing down their dream team to-do list, you'll want to read some aloud. This also helps spark more ideation.

The most important thing during this exercise is creating a space where the team feels comfortable sharing ideas candidly. When I led welcoming ministries at my church, we had a tight budget; however, each year our executive pastor would tell us to dream big and write it all down. His philosophy was that we could always get creative about finding funding sources if we knew what we were working on, but that if we never even put it out there, we wouldn't know to look for ways to fund it. That has always stuck with me. He never promised everything would be funded, either. He just wanted to make sure our creativity wasn't stifled by limiting beliefs.

Once all the ideas are out, you can begin grouping them. This is why I prefer sticky notes, as you can simply move them around. Ask the team what major themes they see amongst the ideas. Group the sticky notes within each theme. There might be a couple of outliers and that's okay.

If you're doing this at a company-wide level, example buckets of goals might be:

- Operations

- People Development

- Innovation

- Collaborations

- Client/Customer Success

- Revenue Generation

When you're working at a departmental level, they will be more granular, while also laddering up to the broader organization-wide goals. For this reason, this process works best when you have clarity and direction from the executive team first.

Once you have defined the buckets of work, you can begin to prioritize the goals within each bucket. At this point in the exercise, some people might start to feel overwhelmed, as there are likely more ideas than capacity. This is a good time to take a break and come back with fresh eyes. I never said this would be a quick, easy process. Much like reorganizing your closet, this can get messy before it all comes together neatly.

Trust yourself. Trust your team. Trust the process.

Invite the team to keep the conversation going by asking their thoughts on which goals should be prioritized and why. You'll want this to align with the mission statement and support what came out of the SWOT analysis. The strengths and opportunities are areas to build upon to optimize the present. The weaknesses and threats are areas to course correct in the future. Take this into account as you're prioritizing goals.

Often, some goal buckets expand on the previous year's accomplishments. If something worked well, don't discount it; not every idea on the board needs to be a brand-new one to move work forward. Sometimes consistency and continuity are your top goals for the year.

Be sure to take a picture of the board so you can have it transcribed later. Bonus points if you want to use the photo to celebrate the team's accomplishment of getting through the exercises together.

If you're on a smaller team, you can wrap this up by assigning milestones to the goals and naming the person responsible for each. This part might be addressed later or in one-on-one meetings.

Adapt this process to your team's working style. You can do it virtually or in person, in one session with breaks or across multiple sessions. The most crucial part is clearly explaining each step to bring everyone with you throughout the process, ensuring their thoughts are heard.

Individual Joy Blueprint

The Individual Joy Blueprint is a guide to help you communicate, collaborate, and celebrate each other better. You might have seen variations of this, but at its core, the version I developed is refreshed from the viewpoint of joy.

Knowing your team is essential; however, we are all human, and the human brain has certain capacity levels, making it hard to remember everything about everyone. Additionally, the invention of social media has introduced increased levels of connections beyond what is neurologically typical. Think about it this way: You used to solely interact with your family, neighbors, and co-workers, but now it's you, them, plus the plethora of online interactions that come at you from a million different directions.

Use the Individual Joy Blueprint as your cheat code. After this activity, ask the team to share what's on their Individual Joy Blueprint. Hearing it out loud and having the opportunity to discuss commonalities in real time reinforces your memory around it. Save this in a common space for the team to access. I like to go back to these anytime I'm leading a "difficult conversation," so we both have space to bring our best selves to the conversation.

This is an activity for the team to do annually at the off-site, as well as a way to welcome new joiners throughout the year. Since everyone at the off-site gets to share out loud, I recommend giving new joiners the same opportunity during their first team meeting. Alternatively, you could leverage the individual joy blueprint to welcome them to the team. Be sure to share the folder with everyone else's blueprint so they don't feel like they're the only ones being vulnerable.

Step 4: Assemble Team Toolkit

Once the offsite is complete, your leadership work ramps up. It's your responsibility to assemble a team toolkit. You might not physically assemble it yourself, as you may have support staff for that, but you still have to prioritize it.

It's important to follow through on all that was ideated and shared during the previous steps. This is how you build trust with your team: they'll have confidence that you not only heard their thoughts but also that an entire ecosystem was constructed collaboratively. This is not a promise that every single thought or word is included. This is a promise that everything was taken into consideration and synthesized into the best possible outcome to support the whole team's work in alignment with the broader organization's work.

Your team toolkit will include the following:

1. Team Mission Statement

2. Team Accomplishments

3. Team Goals (in buckets and prioritized within the buckets)

4. Individual Joy Blueprints

The toolkit is key for continuity as the team can reference it at any time. You'll want to save this in a shared drive for ease of access. I love slide decks, so I typically organize the mission statement, accomplishments, and goals into a brief deck. The individual joy blueprints do not belong in the deck. They are standalone files for each person saved in a single folder in the shared drive.

Step 5: Empower Your Team

You collaborated with the team, and the heavy lifting is complete. Now is the time to support your team in being comfortable sharing their mission, bragging about their accomplishments, and communicating the goals to internal and external stakeholders.

If you created a slide deck, host a team meeting and walk them through it. Show them that you've created talking points for each part, and tell them the talking points are simply a guide to make it easier for them, but that they are the experts and can adjust them to fit their presentation style.

This takes me back to my time at the global aerospace company when I led the strategic refresh of a global program that had been in existence for decades. At the conclusion of that project, I collaborated with key stakeholders to create a deck that I then trained over 20 teammates at various locations on. The ripple effect was that they could then share it with hundreds of their local teams. The key to this was understanding that it's not about me and that I didn't have to be the sole person disseminating information across an enterprise. The team's input was accounted for at every step, and they were proud of the outcome. It was their turn to shine when they shared the updates with peers from different functions. I might have led the charge on that restructuring project, but together we saved the company $2M annually, significantly reduced compliance risk, and increased operational efficiency. I can't lie to you and say it started out roses. There was a lot of skepticism surrounding the project in the beginning, which is normal for any major change. The important part is that by the end, we had something everyone could enjoy.

When teams have doubts and confusion about their work and how it connects to their team, they're not comfortable discussing it in meetings or at networking events. When you lead with joy and purpose, you eliminate the confusion and replace it with confidence.

One of your goals as a purpose-driven leader is to instill confidence and pride in the team. Clarity does this for you.

PART III

JOY JUMPSTART

Ask a colleague to meet you for coffee, with the pretext that you want to be intentional about team goals and wins by discussing them. Providing a pretext is important so they don't feel caught off guard during your coffee chat.

During your coffee chat, **lead by sharing that you want to hear their thoughts** on what they thought was the team's most significant win over the last few months, and that you'll reciprocate in sharing what you thought it was, too.

Let the conversation flow naturally from there. Maybe even pose a question to them about how their team's work supports company goals. Get curious with your teammate.

PART III

CHAPTER 8

Lead in a Way People Want to Follow

You're walking in your purpose, protecting your joy at work, so now you are officially ready to serve as a joy agent in the office. This leadership role isn't based on title, salary, or whether you're exempt or non-exempt. It is purely based upon your ability to lead with joy.

When we looked at the four key areas of life, we saw how the different aspects spill over into one another. As you choose a joy-centered life, it will be contagious to others.

This is a fun position and one that can have ripple effects on your career. There's always going to be tough times at work, but it's your reaction to those times that makes you stand out.

THE SUPERPOWER OF JOY-BASED LEADERSHIP

There is a shift that happens when you've learned how to protect and spread joy at work. You stop performing leadership and start practicing it. You stop reacting to every fire and start choosing how you show up. You realize leadership is not about being louder, more authoritarian, or more impressive. It is about being grounded enough that people feel safe, seen, and steady around you. That is the moment when joy stops being personal and starts becoming communal.

So many people talk about "scaling" in business. Well, your own personal joy journey has a way of scaling in the workplace.

When you're carrying the invisible load of professional expectation, personal responsibility, and the exhausting pressure to prove yourself worthy of the seat you're sitting in, sometimes you can become focused almost too much on the usual models of "power." Don't fall for it!

We've been sold very limited versions of leadership. Most of them focus on authority, efficiency, dominance, or performance. The headlines celebrate the ruthless and the visionaries who sacrificed everything. Very few talk about what it feels like to be led by joy. Fewer still talk about what kind of leader people willingly follow when no one is forcing them to comply.

Joy helps. And I'm not talking about the shallow, forced "we're a family" messages that workplaces throw around. Real joy creates real connections.

So many people are watching what you do and say, again, no matter where you sit on the corporate ladder, and who is influenced by you. Implementing The Stay Joyful Method becomes a blueprint and informal mentoring.

When your leadership is rooted in joy, people do not follow you out of fear of consequences. They follow you because they trust your presence. They show up more fully because you've shown them what it looks like to be whole at work.

They take greater risks because you've created conditions where a mistake or failure is simply information. They stay because you've made them feel something leadership rarely delivers. They stay because you've made them feel safe. This is true leadership in action, which is hard to measure; however, it is evident in team members as they begin to mirror your leadership behavior.

Joy as a Leadership Strategy: The Science

Joy-driven leadership begins with a simple but radical belief: How people feel at work matters. I see this as a strategic advantage.

Teams do not burn out because they work hard. Your teams will work hard regardless. They burn out because they feel unseen, unsafe, and disconnected while doing hard things. Joy does not eliminate pressure, deadlines, or difficult conversations. It changes how those moments are carried out. Centering joy transforms a burden into a shared challenge and a space for collaboration.

You have probably seen this difference play out, maybe in yourself.

During turbulent times, some people become terse, impatient, and brittle. Their stress leaks into every interaction. A simple question becomes confrontational. A missed deadline becomes a character assessment. Their anxiety is contagious, and suddenly, everyone is operating from fear.

Those who have found and know how to guard joy remain light without being reckless or getting pulled into the drama. They're calm but not checked out and able to hold space for difficulty without drowning in it.

Those are the people others gravitate toward. Those are the leaders people choose to follow.

Joy gives leaders internal stability. That stability becomes a signal to others that this is a safe place to think clearly, speak honestly, and do meaningful work.

Presence Is the First Act of Leadership

One of the simplest and most overlooked acts of leadership is presence. This won't require you to stock up on a bunch of continuing education credits or professional development. But it will call on you to draw upon your own inner well of joy.

Presence looks like greeting people, making eye contact, saying good morning, and meaning it. You ask how someone is doing and actually listen to the answer instead of only waiting for your turn to talk about your own day.

Presence looks like showing up on time to meetings and putting the phone away. It looks like remembering the details people told you weeks ago and asking follow-up questions. It feels like *being* in the room you're in.

It is shocking how rare this has become.

In many workplaces, people pass each other in elevators, hallways, and meetings without acknowledging one another. Everyone is busy, being as "productive" as possible. Despite being connected through laptops, phones, and all the tech gadgets, people somehow remain very disconnected.

Humans are wired for recognition and belonging. When those needs go unmet, people withdraw and try to protect themselves. They eventually stop offering their best ideas because that requires vulnerability, and vulnerability requires safety.

Lifting people does not require grand gestures. Sometimes it starts with a greeting. A smile. A pause. A moment of recognition that says, "I see you. You matter before you produce anything for me."

Presence creates trust because it signals respect. It tells people they are not just resources, but they're part of a relationship.

In a world where most leaders are overbooked and distracted, your full attention is an act of rebellion. Use it.

One of the most powerful ways joy shows up in leadership is through advocating and championing others. You do not need formal authority to be a champion. You do not need to control budgets, nor do you have to be the person who signs off on approvals. All you need is awareness and intention. Joy-based leaders lead others into a path of stronger leadership by discovering their own centers of joy.

A BCG study conducted with over 11,000 workers showed that workers identified "doing work I enjoy" as the factor with the third-strongest correlation with retention at the one-year mark, behind only job security and feeling respected at work.[1]

While some may perceive joy as a soft skill, this clearly shows the correlation between retention and professional joy as a must-have in the workplace. As leaders, you need to cultivate an environment that's primed for joy not only to exist but to thrive. Normalizing conversations around joy within your team is a great way to begin building an environment with trust and engagement.

In fact, in Gallup research conducted by Jim Harter, PhD, we learn that when companies focus on well-being and engagement (conditions where joy is more likely), they see the following:

- Seventy percent higher overall well-being among employees

- Higher organizational citizenship, wherein people voluntarily go above and beyond

- Significantly reduced turnover costs[2]

Other research has found that joyful workplace cultures reduce burnout and enhance productivity.[3,4]

The point? As a leader, you can leverage joy to combat staff turnover, which directly impacts your financial bottom line.

The Individual Joy Blueprint: A Practical Tool for Scaling Connection

All of this sounds amazing in theory, right? But you know me by now. Let's break it down in practical terms that you can actually put to use.

One of my favorite ways to operationalize joy in leadership is through a tool I call the Individual Joy Blueprint, which I introduced in Chapter 7. The Individual Joy Blueprint helps teams understand one another beyond job descriptions. It creates shared language around how people work, connect, and feel valued. It removes assumption and replaces it with clarity. It has two parts.

PART III

The first is "How I Work and Connect." This focuses on working environments, communication styles, collaboration preferences, and boundaries. It answers questions people often assume instead of asking.

Do you prefer written communication or video calls? Are you energized by collaboration or drained by constant interruption? Do you think out loud, or do you need time to process? What does a reasonable boundary look like for you? When are you most creative? How do you prefer feedback, immediate or batched? Are you morning energy or evening energy?

The second part is "What Drives and Inspires Me." This explores recognition preferences, motivators, gratitude language, purpose, and growth goals. How do you like to be recognized, publicly or privately? What kinds of work energizes you? What are you building toward? What would it look like for you to feel truly valued here? What does growth mean to you?

This is not fluff or about being "nice." It provides guidance on navigating interpersonal communication and teamwork.

When teams understand how each person operates best, friction decreases and empathy increases. You stop taking things personally because you know the communication style behind them. You stop assuming someone is disengaged because you know that they think before they speak. You stop feeling hurt by someone's directness because you know it is not meant to come across as harsh or mean.

I experienced this firsthand while managing a global team across multiple time zones. With team members spread across India, the U.S. West Coast, East Coast, and Midwest, scheduling meetings was always going to be challenging. Time zones are not negotiable. But preferences can be understood. Instead of assuming preferences, I asked.

Tataji, one of my direct reports, and I had a simple conversation. Morning or night? He shared that he was a night owl. He preferred working with his local team during the day, taking a break to run and have dinner with his family, then meeting with the U.S.-based team and me in the evening. Our time difference was ten and a half hours. That meant the team and I met with him when it was morning time for us.

It worked beautifully. Now, if I had assumed that Tataji preferred morning meeting times, I would have disrupted the very thing that allowed him to be present at work while also unnecessarily extending my workday. He might have stayed in the role and hit targets, but I just know something essential would have dimmed. Instead, by intentionally acknowledging his preferences, the work didn't suffer. If anything, it improved.

This is the secret that high-performing teams know: Connections like these are what make work possible.

PART III

That small act of respect allowed him to show up as his best self. It strengthened our working relationship. We met goals, AND we built trust. Years later, our professional relationship became personal. I eventually met him and his wife in person, and she thanked me for supporting him in ways that honored their family life. She understood that his work life was not separate from his home life but was an integrated part of it. Respecting one part meant respecting the other.

That is joy-based leadership in action.

Often, when organizations hire, they're only looking for hard skills and talent. They measure performance with metrics, and don't get me wrong; those things matter. Your team's competence is important, but what often gets overlooked is the interpersonal layer. The invisible connection that determines whether people bring their full selves and effort, or just enough to stay employed.

Sometimes you don't notice a gap until a crisis hits.

The Individual Joy Blueprint is the perfect reference during challenging times and big wins.

The larger the team, the more intentional you need to be about this. You cannot know everyone with the same depth, but you can create systems that make knowing possible.

The Individual Joy Blueprint can be introduced at offsites, annual meetings, or during onboarding. New team members can share theirs as part of their introduction, rather than a standard bio that just lists their job history and credentials. They can be revisited annually because people change. What sustains you this year might not sustain you next year.

Leaders can go deeper with their direct reports and encourage them to do the same with their teams. Because memory is fleeting and intention fades without reinforcement, these documents should live in a shared space. Don't file them away to be gone and forgotten. Keep the insights accessible.

Imagine wanting to recognize someone for a win and quickly checking how they prefer to receive appreciation. Maybe you planned to send a private note, but their blueprint shows they value public acknowledgment. That slight adjustment builds trust and demonstrates that you know them and their joy matters to you. Little things like that go a long way.

Leading with Joy Every Day

I know there are still some of you thinking, *This is way too simple*. I don't want to paint a perfect picture as if leading with joy means you won't experience any challenges or deal with difficult people.

Like everything we've talked about, you get to choose joy in these moments, and that is a very empowering feeling.

Even when you feel like you've messed up, you know you were aiming at something with the right intention.

Those who want to lead with joy make it a daily practice, not just a destination you hope to reach one day.

You don't just wait for the "big win" because you find ways to appreciate the small victories and day-to-day projects. You celebrate others' willingness to try something new, even if it didn't work the way you expected.

That daily practice also means honoring boundaries. Protect your calendar as ruthlessly as your stakeholders would protect theirs. This is where things can get awkward. As a leader—I don't care if you're the VP or the EA—you will have to say no. Sure, you may have some late nights, but your joy depends on you leaving at a reasonable hour without guilt. It also means taking vacation and not checking email.

It all boils down to you and you giving your team permission to choose alignment over optics.

Leaders say no to things that look good on paper but feel wrong in their gut. They choose the harder conversation instead of the easier silence. And most importantly, they choose to be honest and authentic rather than perform a version of leadership you think you should be.

When leaders are settled in their joy, they become unbothered in the best way.

JOY JUMPSTART

Take ten minutes to **ponder your recognition style** and how you like to be thanked for a job well done.

Write it down, then **ask a co-worker** what theirs is.

Engage in dialogue about each of your recognition styles and what it looks like in real world application.

JOY THAT ENDURES

JOURNEYS IN JOY: KARINA UNSCRIPTED— FINDING JOY IN THE HARD SEASONS

Karina has not only been a client but also someone with whom I have had the privilege of being on this joy journey for a while.

So, I can tell you that I watched her live by a script she never actually wrote. She was doing everything "right"— the career, the family, the accomplishments—and still felt like a failure on every front.

"I felt constantly in the middle," Karina describes those early years. "If I was doing one thing well, I was doing other things poorly. And usually, I felt like I was doing everything poorly because I couldn't give my best self to everything. I felt like there was maybe something inherently wrong with me or inherently misaligned with the universe in what I was doing."

She was creating evidence of failure in her head while the world looked at her and thought, *She has it all together.*

The difference between those two realities? She didn't know she was writing her own story. She thought she was supposed to be following someone else's.

When Karina pulled out her Joy Bubble from July 2022, finding it again years later in a desk drawer, like a Godwink, something shifted. She realized: I don't get joy from titles. I don't take joy in my kids' grades. I get joy from learning, from accomplishing as a team, and from a little bit of rebellion. From being Karina unscripted.

That's when everything changed.

Not because her life became easier. Life got harder. Her husband Brady's health issues were serious. They moved halfway across the country. Mental health struggles. Physical challenges. Job changes. And yet, Karina kept choosing joy, not as denial, but as intentionality.

"Things have been worse," she says simply. "And I think there's a trust that comes from navigating through big things and coming out well on the other side. But it's also adaptability. It's knowing there's not just one path to success or happiness. There are going to be many paths, and I can find my joy in different places."

These days, Karina is the principal and founder at Jasper Strategy, a visionary PR and marketing firm. She's teaching at Marquette University and has clarity on her next two career steps. Her home is full: a husband who's found his own joy (sparked by hers), two kids growing up knowing their parents enjoy their lives, and four cats.

Her house isn't always perfect. And she's okay with that because she's prioritizing what matters.

"I'm prioritizing this, and this is more important than dust," she laughs. "I've got such a full, wonderful life."

When things feel heavy now—and they still do—Karina knows what to do. She returns to her Joy Bubble. She leans into her "we" (her partnership with Brady). She trusts that there are multiple paths forward. She centers herself in what she knows brings her joy.

She doesn't abandon joy in hard seasons. She holds onto it a little tighter.

Her closing wisdom echoes what we'll discuss next.

"It's your journey. It's not anybody else's. Find your yes."

Karina chose joy while navigating serious health crises, major life transitions, and the beautiful chaos of a full life. You know what? You can, too!

Her experience is living proof that joy isn't something you achieve once. It's something you practice, return to, and choose again, especially when things get hard.

CHAPTER 9

When Fear Shows Up

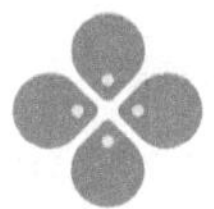

Fear is to be expected. Focus your attention on joy rather than fear to enable action. Fear doesn't belong on your bus, although it will try to get on at every intersection of life.

In a comparative study on emotions, researchers at the School of Medicine, University of California, San Francisco, found that "Positive emotions predicted increases in both resilience and life satisfaction." Furthermore, they assert that "Positive emotions also mediated the relation between baseline and final resilience."[1]

Fear creates undue pressure to make the "right" decision, perform a certain way, and more. Joy makes you more resilient in the face of pressure. In fact, research has found that "Happiness and resilience are closely interconnected, with multiple studies indicating that higher levels of happiness contribute to greater resilience and vice versa.[2]

Resilient people bounce back faster from stress, enabling them to sustain high performance over time rather than burning out.

There will be times when fear will immobilize you and cause you to freeze—everything from brain fog to not even being able to do physical activities. You'll be frozen, which is why it's so hard to choose joy over fear in those moments.

These are the moments you must fight for your joy with every ounce of will in your soul.

This is why it's important to have joy as your foundation.

As someone who's battled depression and anxiety, I've had moments where it's difficult to choose joy because I can barely even remember what joy feels like. That's when I take out my Joy Bubble and pick something from there to do.

Creating a Joy Bubble in the good times means you can always return to it and draw on it to recall what you need to reclaim your joy.

Those moments when you forget what joy is can be the scariest. You lie there in bed, wondering what's next, why you have to get up, and where this is all going.

Those are the moments you need:

- Your Joy Bubble: a reminder of what joy looks like for you.

- Your joy squad: the people in your life who will yank you out of your funk with support, love, and understanding.

- Your Accomplishments Journal: the record book of how fabulous you are that acts as a consummate reminder of what you are undeniably capable of.

Use these tools as your joy jolts to bring you back to you.

I have these moments all the time. People don't think I do because I don't let these moments define me, and I've chosen to learn tactics for working through them. But like most humans, I have these moments because life is tough.

When I moved to Chicago, I didn't land my dream job immediately. I also didn't give up. It took about three years after my move to land my dream role in corporate philanthropy. In that time, I put in the work to get there. The goal was still the same, and my joy was still driving it, which made the grind feel less grimy and more meaningful.

It was three tough years that included being turned down for countless roles and working a job I hated (but knew was a means to my greater purpose). During that period, I engaged in networking with intention and purpose, sharing my story in hopes of being referred for a role. Oftentimes, I felt embarrassed when someone referred me to a job, I interviewed for the role, and then didn't get the position. I was barely making ends meet, and my budget felt like a tightrope walk. In those years, I figured out how to show up as if I were in my future position, even though I didn't have the title yet. Those years of grit prepared me for what was next. Unbeknownst to me, that grit also prepared me for what came after corporate philanthropy: entrepreneurship, writing this book, sharing with you what happens when you let joy lead your goals, networking, and leadership.

Reflecting on that period of my life made leaving my CSR (corporate social responsibility/corporate philanthropy) role quite difficult; however, I can barely imagine life any other way now. You will notice that time can change your entire perspective on a past period of life.

THE "I QUIT" POST

After resigning, I posted on LinkedIn, and the response shocked me—hundreds of comments, DMs, and reactions from people in my network and those I hadn't yet met. I shared with the world that I had left my role and was leaning into my joy...and I didn't know what was next, other than a reset.

I look at that post now, and I'm proud of myself for acting out of joy rather than acting out of fear. I made a joy-based decision when it would have been easier to make a fear-based decision.

Here's what the world didn't know. I had only three months of living expenses saved, one client in my pipeline, and no clue how much entrepreneur health insurance had skyrocketed.

I'm a single Black woman who doesn't come from generational wealth, as in there is ZERO financial support if I need it. We were living in unprecedented times with a terrible job market.

That was the scary list, but there was a joy list the world didn't know about, too....

I had a very strategic business coach who'd reviewed my plans. My therapist had been preparing me mentally. I understood my budget and where I could cut spending. I had a group of business mentors who poured into me regularly, sharing the good, bad, and the ugly of what I needed to do and hear. I had placed myself in entrepreneur and speaker spaces to learn and grow with others. Earlier in the year, I refined the software used in my business to get organized and save money.

On top of all that, we were living in unprecedented times where people craved joy...and I'm The Joy Amplifier™!

Wow, when I write it out like this, I surprise myself because the joy list is actually longer than the scary fear list, but at the time, those fears had me shaking in my boots.

The biggest thing of all is that I had been praying (no, *begging*) God for clarity on what to do, yet when I got that clarity, I was scared to act on it. I sat there joking that,

"God must want me to go hungry!" but I quickly learned that was not the case at all.

What happened next?

Four epic events set off my career transition and led me to decide not to apply for W-2 roles.

One. I received a DM from a consultant who produced the annual conference for a global fast-food company. He'd seen my LinkedIn posts about joy, checked out the workshop offering on my website, and was requesting two workshops.

Two. I spoke at the Chicagoland Chamber of Commerce, where the publicity, coupled with support, garnered me new clients and exposure to my ideal clients.

Three. I kicked off the #BeyondTheBadge campaign to build meaningful connections before, during, and after the Association for Talent Development (ATD) conference. My conference goals were to learn, meet clients, and be selected to speak the following year, all of which have come to fruition.

Four. I negotiated and signed my first contract for a series of workshops rather than a single workshop.

Wow, I guess God showed me...She didn't want me to go hungry....She wanted me to have room to grow and glow. I was mind-blown.

I'm not saying to quit your job tomorrow. Entrepreneurship is the hardest thing I've ever done, and it's not for everyone. What I am suggesting is that you be intentional about aligning your life with your joy so that you can make strategic risks that minimize your fear.

Fear didn't mean I was off-track. It meant my mind needed to catch up with my reality.

Leaning into my joy rather than my fears led to the most significant strategic business decision of my life. But the thing is, I was ready.

I was ready because I'd been testing various offers for over four years, collecting client feedback through surveys to improve, and paying close attention to people's reactions when I talked about my business, which enabled me to refine my messaging.

I leaned into my purpose (overlap of joy and skills) by removing offers that didn't bring me joy. My joy squad was assembled and ready to spread the word that Goal and Grind was open and available for work!

As I look back at the "I quit" post, I see constants and parallels in my journey moving to Chicago, my current journey, and the journey you'll inevitably embark upon.

Joy doesn't come without challenges, obstacles, or, as corporate America would say, "opportunities."

You can have more than one dream job. The critical piece is how and when you'll pour into each one. Corporate social responsibility is as much my dream job as entrepreneurship; they just occurred in different phases of my life and brought me joy in ways both similar and distinct.

Tenacity and showing up will take you far in life. If you want people to think of you in a certain role, you need to speak it and do it all the time. On average, it takes someone hearing something over seven times to remember it. That means you need a combination of telling someone in person, email, and/or via social posts seven times before they fully remember what you're trying to do. I started saying I was a motivational speaker and corporate trainer long before it was my full-time role, which is why so many people said "Finally!" rather than "What is that?" or "Why are you doing that?" The transition made sense, and they didn't need to question it as it was a natural progression.

Show up! Showing up is half the battle. You will stand out when you show up because most people don't make the time to show up. It's not enough to just say you're good at something. Start doing it so you can truly speak to it with deeper knowledge and understanding. It's very easy to spot someone who doesn't really know or understand what they're talking about, but if you let your curiosity take over, then you'll learn from others, try things out for yourself, and make improvements.

Networking with purpose, intention, and joy is a true differentiator. When I was pouring into my CSR pivot, I networked in CSR spaces with CSR practitioners. As I pivoted to a full-time entrepreneur focused on authorship, speaking, and training, I networked in speaker, training, and entrepreneur spaces, as well as in the spaces where my target clients were. I've had fun learning in each space, conversing, and getting creative on how to solve problems.

Transferable skills are a real thing. It can be hard to see them, but believe me, they're there. Leverage your Accomplishments Journal to identify your transferable skills. Have it out next to you as you go through job descriptions for your next dream role to support you in identifying skill similarities. Take for example, if you're in sales, you likely have great people skills and the ability to get a group of stakeholders on board with an idea; thus you would be able to apply those to skills in a field such as change management where you need the ability to leverage creative thinking and problem solving skills to get a group of stakeholders bought in on upcoming changes.

Looking at me as an example, I can't even count the number of times I've shared something about the business with my mom and she'll say "Oh, you learned that when you were at the software company!" or "I remember you doing something similar to that at the aerospace company...it prepared you for where you are now!" Every professional experience has built who I am, how I show up, and my thought processes.

Friend Quotient

Fear can make us think we need lots of friends, lots of money, lots of appointments on our calendar, lots of everything. You name it, we think we need a lot of everything, but that's just not true.

Take your friend group as an example. Five uplifting friends can do wonders for your quality of life, from laughing together to thinking through tough situations together; they bring you joy. However, on the flip side, ten draining friends will suck your energy and detract from what the five uplifting friends bring to the table. That's why there's the saying, "a few bad apples ruin it for us all."

Uplifting friends in your joy squad are those who give you positive energy, solutions, thought leadership, and raise your spirit. Draining friends in your joy squad are those who give you negative energy, plant seeds of doubt, and exhaust your soul.

This theory is even mathematically correct, which kind of blows my mind.

Quick friend math: Uplifting friends are positive numbers, and draining friends are negative numbers.

$$+5 \text{ friends}$$
$$\underline{-10 \text{ friends}}$$
$$-5 \text{ total friends}$$

Five uplifting friends are a positive number, and ten draining friends are a negative number. When you add them up, you get a sum of five draining friends, meaning if you're focused on quantity, you'd take those ten draining friends, even though they literally bring down your total friend quotient. But when you focus on quality, you'll be content and enriched by the five uplifting friends.

That means you could have fifteen people on your joy squad, but since ten of them are poisoning your mind with negative energy, they outweigh and overshadow those five people who nourish your mind with positive energy.

Whether you're making a personal or professional decision, if you make it rooted in joy rather than based in fear, you can't go wrong, as you'll be choosing yourself and your unique joy.

A few reflection questions for you to apply this to your life:

- How can you get curious and learn about your future role today?

- How can you start showing up as your future role today?

- How can you be intentional and build your network around your future role today?

Move in the Midst of Fear

Fear doesn't disqualify you.

Fear is normal. It's about how you handle fear energy so that it doesn't consume you. It's about recognizing when fear shows up and knowing how to move in the midst of it.

The funny thing about fear is that it has a way of disguising itself as responsibility, logic, and "the right next step." It whispers that stability is safety and that deviation is danger. But joy doesn't disappear in the presence of fear. It waits for movement anyway. The truth is, learning how to move while afraid is often the very doorway to rediscovering what lights you up.

Choosing joy is rarely about having perfect certainty. It's about making decisions that may go against everything you've always known. It's about honoring a quiet truth inside you, even when that truth breaks from the expected script.

Fear is simply an indicator that you've come upon a fork in the road where you get to make a decision. Remember that joy is a choice just as much as fear. Give yourself grace as it takes time, practice, and a renewed commitment to your joy to continue implementing this mindset shift.

JOY JUMPSTART

Think about one fear that's creating a barrier to forward movement in your life.

What's something you've been wanting to do or a step you've been thinking about taking, but fear has been holding you back? Is it applying for that job? Asking for a raise? Moving across the country? Cutting ties with a draining friend?

Imagine how your life might change if you focus on joy rather than fear to finally take that step.

Write a letter to your future self, describing what your life is like after taking that specific action and, ultimately, choosing joy over fear.

CHAPTER 10

Holding Joy in Hard Seasons

Joy doesn't always come easily, and anyone who tells you it does hasn't really lived. There are times when choosing joy seems impossible, yet those are the times you might need it the most. This is why setting a foundation of joy is vital.

That consistently electing situations that can generate positive emotions leads to greater levels of positive emotions which then promote well-being.

According to Cohn et al., "It is in-the-moment positive emotions, and not more general positive evaluations of one's life, that form the link between happiness and desirable life outcomes."[1] I found this interesting because it shows that even if you don't have consistently positive emotions, including joy, moments of joy can still have a positive effect on your life. We don't have to be perfect all the time. When you are in a hard season of life, use spurts of joy to turn your outlook around.

When you truly know your joy, you can call upon it.

I first learned this in elementary school after the 1995 bombing of the Alfred P. Murrah Federal Building in Oklahoma City. I was in the fifth grade, and my mom came to visit me at school. She said she was there to say hi and to let me know she loved me. I proceeded to go on about my day, and then my teacher announced that there was a bombing downtown and turned on the news so we could all watch it. Everyone in class was sad and worried because our parents all worked downtown, and no one knew who was alive or not. This was long before cell phones and even pagers.

I wasn't worried about my mom's safety because she'd just come to give me a surprise hug and hello. I remember not paying attention to the news because it was the same story over and over again. It was way too graphic for a fifth grader, and to this day, I can't believe my teacher wheeled out that tiny, grainy TV and played it all day long. I haven't visited the bombing site as it was just too much for me.

I do know all the facts about the Oklahoma City bombing but have chosen to protect my joy by not engulfing my life in it because that's what Timothy McVeigh (a white American service award-winning Army veteran) wanted by designing and detonating a bomb that killed 168 people, which included 16 children.

I can't give that man the satisfaction of taking up more of my brain space. My mom's office was a mere few blocks from the federal building, and every time someone brings up the OKC bombing, I'm grateful that my mom visited me at school after the bombing but before my teacher turned on the news. That was my first lesson in watching the news once for data and not re-watching it to traumatize myself. This is how I know that joy is your psychological safety weapon, which you can call upon at any time.

Historical moments are a powerful reminder of what the world is capable of and also what we (as a community and individually) are capable of in the face of tragedy.

In her summer 2009 poem "The Telly Cycle," Toi Derricotte wrote that "Joy is an act of resistance."[2] When I sit with this, I understand it as joy being the one resource that cannot be stolen from us. From the transatlantic slave trade to modern-day robbing of Black creativity, our joy remains our constant. Scientifically, when joy is postponed, your ability to connect, lead, and form community is also delayed. Consider who stands to gain from halting or deferring your joy. The embodiment of joy is a key thread in our ability to resist oppression. Consider how the world has been organized to train natural innovators within the culture to hide their creativity. It is simply another attempt to withdraw one's joy. I lift up and celebrate your joy—past, present, and future—as I know it can (and will) sustain you.

We can wake up and realize it's time to choose joy and drive out the oppressive actions against us. Being a

Black woman in corporate America—well in America in general—has always meant a separate set of unspoken rules. I haven't done a good job of living by those, and honestly, it makes me giggle.

Joy is the greatest defense in the face of marginalization. Just think for a moment, how offhand it is that someone who doesn't even know you spends time hating you. On the one hand, it is scary, but I also love how collectively we, as Black people, have chosen to find humor and tell jokes within the stories of our own enslavement.

In my spare time, I do stand-up comedy. I have a set about my name and what happens when people hear it. Particularly, I once attended a luncheon, and while checking in, the woman at the registration table asked what my name means and where it's from.

I joke that I oblige by sharing with her that it's African and means "born on Sunday," while my inner thoughts know that's not something she would ask someone named Jamie. I go on to share that after learning my name has African roots, she asks how my family got to America, to which I simply reply, "slavery" with a very calm, even keel tone of voice.

The woman proceeds to act as though she's never met a descendant of enslaved people and goes on about how hard that must have been, at which point I interrupt her and remind her that I need my name tag and that she needs to direct me to my corporate sponsor table.

The audience always explodes into laughter when I say "slavery" because it's so unexpected, but it is the honest truth. I am a descendant of enslaved people, and that is how my maternal family came to America. However, I incur regular encounters where my history has been erased so much that people are shocked by the term *slavery*.

That in and of itself is an aggression against my ancestors and me that I've chosen to combat with joy and laughter, and if we're being honest, I make some folks think while I'm at it. My mom describes my comedy as factual accounts of aggressions that I've turned into jokes palatable for all to hear and learn from.

Even if you don't relate to my exact experience, you likely know the feeling of being disregarded or seen by someone as unimportant. While they are responsible for their action, you have agency over your reaction, meaning you can decide how to use your joy in problematic situations.

Humor is a chosen response, not a dismissal.

We are all unique. Joy is not a constant requirement; it's simply not sustainable; however, joy can be a response to imperialism. And since joy looks different for each of us, the response will vary as well. Maybe you reflect on the harm others have done to you through painting, meditation, journaling, or something I haven't named. Whatever the action, it is yours to use. As Beyoncé would say, "The best revenge is your paper," meaning the best revenge is about achieving financial prosperity, and I certainly leverage that joy factor from time to time as well.

Joy Bubbles exist for moments like this.

The moment ends, but then what? It's natural for instances like this to replay in your mind over time (at times unexpectedly). This is why I am proactive about my joy. Naming my joy, sharing it with others, and nurturing it help me prepare my whole psyche (mental and physical) for the flashbacks.

JOY IN GRIEF

I must admit, choosing joy during grief is one of the most difficult things one can do. Consider giving oneself immense grace and gratitude.

Even in the hardest of times, it is possible to remember you still deserve joy, even if it's just a tiny glimmer. Surrounding yourself with people who are a safe space can be a reminder to give yourself permission to reconnect with your joy by understanding it.

I battle with depression, so this is a very real thing for me. There are days I wake up and wonder why.

And on those days, I phone a friend—another of the safe spaces to exist without being "on." I hear the voice of someone who brings me joy, and that shocks me back like a jolt of lightning. That's also why I'm clear to my friends that I really enjoy phone calls because there are times I need those calls. As a single woman who's an entrepreneur, life can be emotionally lonely. I might go days without a personal joy connection. Professional joy connections are different because, to a degree, you have to be "on," which is why I treasure the personal ones where you can just kick back and exist. Just as joy is unique to each person, your sense of personal regulation can be as well. While my personal regulation is a phone call, you will want to decipher what your personal method for regulation is.

Grief and Asking for Help

One year, I journaled that my word of the year would be '*help*' because I needed to be better about asking for and receiving help.

I would hear myself on stage saying, "Goal crushing is a team sport," and here it was my turn to listen to my own advice: Ask for help.

I was lost and drowning in my grief journey. Grief removed my sense of connection and belonging. The world as I knew it was different, and who I was changed (or was changing).

The shift to settling into a new me started when I shared with my cleaning lady that my darling fur baby, Chanel, had gone to heaven, and I asked for her help reorganizing my home, plus storing Chanel's belongings.

PART IV

After months of deliberation, I joined a pet loss grief support group that my therapist had shared with me. It was my first experience with a support group. I was scared. But I logged into the virtual support room anyway. I finally saw that I wasn't the only one, as I got to share space with people at various stages of grieving their loss. As I listened to people in the group share, there was a sense of familiarity. I saw what was possible for me, and I heard where I had been.

Another form of support I sought out was collaboration with podcast hosts to create experiences for me to share joy because I missed doing this work.

One of the critical ways I asked for help was in my professional life, as during this time, my virtual assistant knew everything, enabling her to step up and fill in when I couldn't. Megan kept my business alive even when I didn't ask her to.

Unbeknownst to me, that journal entry about my word of the year, *help*, was preparing me for our annual Vision and Goals Party. At the event, a conversation sparked about asking for help and what that means to the person you ask. It was a beautiful discussion, exploring the honor of being respected and trusted enough to receive a request for help. It wasn't until I started writing this book that I realized the connection to my prior journaling.

What do you need help with this year? Make this something you ask yourself at the beginning of each year or each transition in life (because they don't always happen at the beginning of the year).

Joy in Rejection

When I started writing this book, I went through my journal entries from past years and found something very interesting: I journaled about rejection a ton.

We will all be rejected at some point.

It sucks, but it's part of life. It will hurt to varying degrees, but what I now know about rejection is that the more you understand your joy and are in community with the joy squad aligned with it, the easier it is to manage rejection. Reading those journal entries, I re-felt the pain of each rejection deeply, but then I realized I had chosen not to let that rejection define me.

I recently had someone tell me they didn't think I had experienced rejection. The ironic part is that I have been rejected. I just choose not to let rejection define me, overwhelm me, consume my thoughts, become a reflection of who I am, or stop me from progressing. I chose to define my story, my path, and myself. That is likely why this person had the notion that I had never been rejected.

Focusing on joy means rejection doesn't define you; it's just a footnote in your life's story. A footnote so tiny that people will think you've never experienced it.

Own your rejection so you can heal and move forward from it. Some rejection doesn't even have to do with you because it's all about the person or persons rejecting you. Imagine walking around with the luggage of everyone who has ever rejected you. It's heavy! And that emotional weight can and will cause doubt and fear in your life, which squelches your joy.

That's why I re-read *The Four Agreements* annually as a reminder that I don't need to make assumptions of why someone is rejecting me because it's none of my business, and it will only drive me insane and consume my thoughts.

I think Tamron Hall said it best when I saw her speak: "They will make you not even recognize yourself if you let them."

That's the power of the tongue that Don Miguel Ruiz references in *The Four Agreements*, and it's exactly why I had to decide that my joy was worth more than my rejection from various aspects of society. Ruiz's notion of not making assumptions and being cautious with your words combines into a type of mental protection against spiraling. When you don't make assumptions, your mind is cleared of "What did they mean by that?" thinking patterns. Being kind with your words means you don't become the person who causes doubt and fear in others. You can build community with harmony, living out these principles.

The gossipers don't deserve the ability to squelch your joy, so don't let them. From here on, make rejection a footnote (not a highlight). Focus so much on your joy that it becomes your shield.

Rejection became my protection. At every turn, it's true. Rejection is my protection. I was repeatedly rejected from

CSR roles I applied for in Oklahoma City. A list of companies too long for me to even recall. You name it, they said no. And thank God they did because I never would have moved if I could have gotten my dream job in OKC. So, I left, and when I got to Chicago, I landed my dream job in CSR at Fortune 100 companies—global companies far beyond the ones who rejected me in Oklahoma City.

That rejection not only protected me, BUT it catapulted me into the woman I am today.

The space to dream bigger was provided by those very rejections from job applications. Rejection gave me the opportunity to move to my dream city, fly higher, and was essentially my freedom ticket. I am so thankful for that rejection.

Forms of Rejection

There are many types of rejection, from emotional rejection to professional, familial, and even self-rejection. Rejection is all around us. The thing to focus on is making an effort to choose joy in the face of rejection. Choosing yourself in the face of rejection and seeing it as a potential blessing, protection, and redirection.

Your response to rejection is yours to make, not the rejector. It can be paralyzing, but you have tools in your Joy Bubble to determine what energy you feed rejection as well as the person, process, or thing that initiated your rejection.

Younger me didn't know I was being rejected, so I did nothing but cry when I was bullied. College me felt it more; she was sick of it, so she was sassy, sharp-witted, and snapped back. Post-college baby Bose was surprised as it was familiar but somehow unexpected, so she was all over the place, sometimes confused and other times lighting a match of Scorpio fury. Adult me is more measured, rarely giving energy to rejection as I've come to expect that it will happen. I don't know when it will happen, but I know it is a possibility; therefore, when it does, I look to the next option that awaits me. Throughout life, you might also go through phases of your reaction to rejection, which is normal.

The Best "No" of My Life!

When I first got to Chicago, I was desperate for work. I always told myself that if I didn't find a job and make enough money, then I'd get "sent back" to Oklahoma, where at least I knew I had enough people in my network to help me get a job. I was determined not to get sent back!

I was introduced to a woman who led a family foundation dedicated to breast cancer research. She was looking for a development professional who serves as the main fundraiser for a nonprofit organization. I did not want to return to fundraising at a nonprofit, but I took the conversation with her because I was desperate for work.

We met at Starbucks on what seemed like my first big Chicago snow. We had a lovely conversation, and I learned about the foundation and how it honored her late mother. It's a beautiful, impactful organization. At the end of our conversation, she told me she wasn't going to hire me. The greatest part was that she said she thought I was meant for something more—a bigger job. I was kind of shocked that she not only knew that but also had the guts to say it out loud. She saw me! Like, she really saw me, and I've been grateful for that over the years. She even offered to drive me home because of the snow. If I'd gone to work for her as a fundraiser, I would have been back in the same job that I left in Oklahoma City, the same job I'd set out to pivot away from. After that, we stayed in touch, and I focused more on the type of role I had set out to pivot toward. I'll never know for sure what would have happened if she offered me that job, but my guess is that I would have raised a bunch of money (since I was good at that), gotten comfortable, and never gone after my dream job in CSR. This is how rejection can change your entire trajectory for the better.

Getting a "No" Helped Me Grow

I got to practice my pitch and fine-tune how I would do it. Just think, if you get hired after every interview, you never really get to practice your interview skills in a live setting. Sure, you can practice with a coach, mentor, or friend, but that will never have the same energy or pressure as a real, live interview.

I gained clarity on my target audience. As an entrepreneur, I learn much more when I pitch a potential client and get a no, because afterward I think about why I got the no and how I can do better next time. I have a deeper understanding of what they're looking for and what they're not looking for by listening deeply and asking questions about the no. No doesn't mean the conversation is over. It's simply a redirection of the conversation's end goal.

The Sad Jar

Sometimes, you just have to put things in your Sad Jar and keep it moving. I'm not saying you'll never address it, but maybe it's too much for you at the moment, which is okay for you to recognize, set a boundary, and commit to picking it up later when you are in a place to work through it. There was a very clear and definitive moment when I came to understand this concept.

I was on a virtual session with my therapist when I found myself being asked to dig deeper. I wasn't ready. My mind couldn't do it and neither could my heart. I heard a voice ask me something, and I said no. No, I couldn't go there; I just couldn't. So, I looked up at the screen and asked, "Can we put that in my Sad Jar?"

I created the term *Sad Jar* to describe a container of emotional blocks to work through when you have the emotional bandwidth.

When my therapist asked me to go deeper, I knew I had to go there, but today just wasn't the day.

I have a very unique therapist (or at least I think I do). She believes in continued progress and growth, just like I do, so when we complete something, she wants me to consider what I want to work on next and might ask if it's time to take something out of my Sad Jar. She makes space for me to select what's coming out of the jar to work on and keeps me accountable to working on something, no matter how big or small it is.

So, when I asked my therapist, "Can we put that in my Sad Jar?" she said yes. But I also knew that meant I had to let her know when "that" would be resurfacing, emerging from the Sad Jar when I was mentally and emotionally ready. She understood. She respected this, but she never forgets the contents of my Sad Jar.

You can use a Sad Jar as a useful boundary-setting tool for emotional protection and growth. You can create one as your emotional bookmark for things you want to revisit later, so you can decide when the time is right for the emotional labor.

Calling Upon Your Joy

We will all have bad days, but imagine what it would be like to work through those days if you already have a Joy Bubble? That's when you go to your Joy Bubble and identify something you can do for yourself. It can be small and simple or large and extravagant. The only thing that matters is that it was in your Joy Bubble and you're doing it for you. Remove what is crushing your soul and replace it with something from your Joy Bubble. You are essentially squelching something that has a negative impact on you with an activity you already know will uplift you. Choosing joy isn't something that happens overnight. It's a lifestyle choice that you have to commit to, nurture, and renew regularly.

My joys are talking with friends and family. So, when things get tough, I start dialing! Anyone who gets regular calls from me in the morning loves it because it's the purest connection. It's before the influences of the outside world begin to creep in and influence our thoughts. It's knowing that I thought of them at the beginning of my day, choosing to have an intentional touch base to see how they're doing, and share how I'm doing, as we value each other's thoughts. It's honestly so fun! Regardless of whether we talk for five minutes or five hours about topics that are light, heavy, or in between, the main thing is our connection.

I must say, this isn't light work; however, honoring yourself even in the darkest, toughest times is a step. It's not about the amount of effort put in. The key is knowing your true joy well enough to call upon it when you need it. It's about granting yourself permission to move in joy through difficult situations. This type of emotional labor takes time and practice. Give yourself space to take that step.

JOY JUMPSTART

Journal for fifteen minutes about what you will do to call upon your joy when it seems impossible. Will you use your own Sad Jar, call a friend, or label a rejection as a footnote in your life story? Is there something from your Joy Bubble that would be useful in honoring how you feel in those moments?

Write down at least two specific actions you will take when you need to hold joy during hard seasons.

CHAPTER 11

Make Joy a Way of Life

My mom is the original joy guardian.

Throughout my childhood, my mom had one goal: for me to know joy. Second to that was instilling in me the belief that I could do anything I wanted. Imagine that: a Black girl growing up in the extremely homogeneous environment of Edmond, Oklahoma, who only knew joy, hope, and endless possibilities.

As an adult, I am beyond grateful that she raised me in a Joy Bubble. One of the first keynotes I gave included audience interaction where I asked the audience to turn to their neighbor and share what brings them joy. Then I asked if anyone would share with the full audience.

The first woman to share said, "No one had ever asked about her joy." I was both saddened and stunned because that was a world I didn't know, a world I never even imagined existed.

I had taken for granted that I grew up with a mother who protected and honored my joy. It was the most important thing to her. That I have joy. Period.

That moment sparked my mission to spread joy to the world!

At every turn in life and with every idea that I brought to my mom, she would ask me how I planned to get there. Not why I wanted to go there.

I would later learn, through professional coach training, the different emotions triggered by the question of "how" versus "why." As an adult and through coaching school, I've learned that it is not the norm for most, as the outer world (including well-intentioned family members) constantly asks why you want to take a certain pathway.

Consider the underlying subtext and signals associated with asking "how" versus 'why'.

Asking someone how...	Asking someone why...
Inspires creativity	Creates doubt
Signals that the person believes you can do it	Signals that the person doesn't think you can do it
Offers support	Offers criticism

When I look back at my life, I'm very grateful for all the times I was asked "how" rather than "why."

Are there times for "why"? Yes, absolutely, but the situational timing of it is everything.

It turns out my mom wasn't just the original joy guardian. She was also a life coach and didn't even know it!

In my forty-one years of life, there is only one time when my mother didn't believe I could do something. She was perplexed that I was taking a comedy class because she claimed, "You're not funny. You're very serious."

Well, her years of being my biggest fan pushed me over the edge into a stand-up comedy performance at Second City, where she got the shock of a lifetime. Her very serious, strategic daughter is, in fact, funny. Not to brag, but I received a standing ovation that night from a room of forty strangers, plus fifteen of my dearest friends.

My mom can literally find joy in the dustiest of situations. I'm not sure how, but she says she's God's favorite. So I've always assumed that's why; however, as an adult, I realize she made a choice for joy as a child, which has carried her through a beautiful existence.

One day, I was frustrated writing this book and I told her this was very hard for me. Her response was, "That's what they say."

I responded, "Who said that?"

She jokingly said, "Anyone who's written a book, and you're confirming it."

I laughed so hard knowing she doesn't know any authors, at which point she said, "Don't you feel better now?"

It's that simple. Mom wanted to alleviate stress, so she was honest, supportive, and joyful. We had a good laugh, and my brain block was removed. I'll never know if she did that on purpose or if she's just always open to letting God work through her, but what I do know is that I'm very lucky to have someone so consistently jovial in my life.

THE THREE Cs OF JOYFUL LIVING

I've given you three main concepts throughout this book, and the underlying connection among them is living with joy, leveraging it as the greatest tool in your toolkit. Joy as your metaphorical compass. It's the invisible thread that binds the Vision and Goals Method™ to the Elevator Pitch and Beyond Method, as well as the Purpose-Driven Leadership Method. Each of these three methodologies uses the power of joy.

You might not remember each methodology in its completeness, but take this with you:

The Three 3Cs of Joyful Living

1. Celebrate your wins.

2. Cheer for others' success.

3. Connect with your community.

These three will support every phase of your journey in joy.

Celebrate Your Wins

There are several times when you can use your Joy Bubble, and this is certainly one of them. Celebrating yourself doesn't have to be a major production, but it does need to be meaningful to you. Wins can be as small as taking a nap or as giant as making *The New York Times* Best Sellers list as they're equally important to building and reviving your joy. Making time to celebrate your wins can be a planned occasion. Take, for example, if you make a weekly appointment with yourself or have a deadline coming up, schedule a moment to celebrate when you hit it. Both can be calendar appointments that include you, or you can invite someone from your joy squad. Regardless of how you celebrate, please make sure you are rewarded for your efforts, as weaving joy throughout your journey is a win in itself. It's easy to think of all the things you haven't gotten done. I invite you to reframe it by regularly acknowledging everything you *have* gotten done.

Cheer for Others' Success

The next C is to cheer for others' success. I've come to realize, the world was not made for us to be individualistic. Building community stems from seeing, hearing, and recognizing those around you. In my workshops,

I sometimes ask people to share an achievement they're proud of. It's inevitably the highest-energy part of the event as everyone claps for them; however, my favorite part is the visible signs of appreciation, mixed with a bit of surprise, as the room cheers for them. You deserve this type of energy, as do we all. Think about the small ways you can incorporate this practice within your own life.

Connect With Your Community

The third C of Joyful Living is to connect with your community. Building true community happens over time, one connection after another. True connection takes work, listening without judgement, and engaging with curiosity. It requires showing that you care about them and seeing how they care for you.

A few years ago, at our annual Vision and Goals Party, a discussion was sparked about asking for help. It was beautiful to hear one woman share how honored she feels when someone asks for her help, as it signals that she's a trusted, valued advisor when someone seeks out her thoughts. This is a form of community building that improves over time in a relationship.

The 3Cs of joyful living is a framework to support you in building an ongoing lifestyle of joy in your relationship with yourself and those around you. Take me as an example. I practice #FinshlineFriday each week.

It's something I started doing on my own as a reminder to celebrate my wins, and now I've made it a weekly communal practice, enabling me to cheer for my community members' success. The bonus is the community connections that are sparked as a result.

GOAL CRUSHING IS A TEAM SPORT

You might have noticed that when you lack clear strategic goals, your community is fuzzy about how best to support you. Imagine if someone offered to support you; however, you couldn't name the support you need.

Lean into your joy squad. Tell them what's going on, what you need, and when you need it.

My joy squad is diverse, all playing a different role and all bringing a different perspective to the table. Together, they make me whole. What does it mean to have a diverse cheering squad? It feels like seeing your community act and move in ways that were shaped by their previous life experiences. You learn from them, and they learn from you.

For instance, if a problem arises with my finances, I go to someone in my financial joy squad; whereas, when I need workout inspiration, I call my friend, Tasha, who has a solid workout routine. At times, the most crucial joy squad is my lawyer besties, whom I reach out to when I need a strategic thought partner, as the law school pedagogy transformed their brains into some of the greatest critical thinkers.

It's awe-inspiring how, over the span of my forty-one years of life, the exact right people are in my life, and we each support each other in unique ways. My joy squad has people from many different backgrounds, ethnicities, sexual orientations, professional sectors, and more. They also live all over the world!

I always say goal crushing is a team sport because nothing that I have done is solely mine. It has been the people who have lifted me up and/or spoken my name in rooms that I wasn't in.

I take that very seriously because it's my job and my duty to also do this for others—lift them up and speak their names in spaces they're not in. You might have noticed this pattern in your own life as well, and you don't have to know right now. But you will know when an opportunity arises for you to uplift someone in your community.

You deserve a balanced life filled with joy and purpose. Creating a lifestyle rooted in joy takes time, practice, commitment, and repetition. Be kind to yourself throughout your journey in joy. Think of the grace you give your closest friend, and then look into a mirror to receive that same grace.

Joy may have been modeled for you. Joy may have been introduced to you. And now, joy is yours to practice in perpetuity.

JOURNEYS IN JOY: HER RISE
TO SUCCESS THROUGH COMMITTING
AND RECOMMITTING TO HER JOY

I've shared several examples of my clients' journeys in joy. I want to share one more with you before we wrap this up. I believe you will be inspired and see how this book is just the beginning.

Sarah Glazer is a powerhouse. Not only is she a mom, daughter, wife, sister, all of the things, but she also works at a Fortune 500 global industrial automation manufacturer. And most importantly, she's what I call one of the OGs, the original Vision and Goals Method™ practitioners, who came to one of my Vision and Goals Parties in the beginning, and they all started implementing this for themselves.

I watched Sarah log into the virtual Vision and Goals Party during the peak of the pandemic with a young toddler at home, mid-career, and a problem she couldn't solve: How do I put it all together?

"There were so many ideas in my mind," Sarah remembers. "I was doing well and enjoying my role for the most part, but something was missing. How do I put it together?"

The Visions and Goals Method™, along with the four key areas, changed everything.

"That framework was so helpful," Sarah says. "It was easy to construct. It was easy to remember. Every few weeks, every few months, I still refer back to that framework."

PART IV

Notice what she said: She still refers back. Not "referred back once." Still. Continuously. As a practice.

This is what joy as a way of life actually looks like.

"I kept that framework in mind, and this foundation of joy is not an endpoint. It's part of the journey. It's part of the process. Remember to have joy in every decision that you make."

When a job opportunity came more than a year after the workshop, Sarah didn't rush. She was on maternity leave. The timing was terrible. But instead of running away from her current role or chasing the first shiny thing, she did something radical: She interviewed them.

"I didn't just run to the first opportunity. I really sat back and thought about the Vision and Goals Party," Sarah explains. "I know what my four goals are within each quadrant. I know what brings me joy. I've spent the time thinking about it. And that thread is what carried me. I find the most fulfillment in those activities that align with the goals that I had set and that are rooted in joy."

She looked at the job description. She had conversations with people at the company. She asked, "Does this align with my values? Does this align with the vision I set for myself?"

Three years later, she's a leader at a Fortune 500 company. But more importantly, she's still practicing the framework.

"I've fulfilled a lot of professional goals," she reflects. "I feel great about it." Then she adds, "I have a beautiful family and they're doing well. So that's in a great spot."

It was lovely to watch Sarah air-draw the boxes of the Conceptualization Chart when describing that she had been focused heavily on the personal and professional key areas of life and is now wanting to focus on the health and financial areas of life.

She continues by sharing, "But now, as I look at that framework, I'm going to focus on my health, and I'm going to focus a little bit more on financial."

The confidence of recognizing her strides, coupled with knowing her goals in all four key areas of life, makes room for peace in understanding when it's time to shift focus to another area for a bit.

Sarah presents an important part of her joy-driven plans: "My financial situation is in pretty good shape, but now I need to optimize because I'm not twenty or twenty-five anymore. And I would like to retire at a decent age. That's where the next transformation and focus is going to be."

This is the evolution of joy as a way of life: You don't master it once. You revisit it. You adjust. You pivot with purpose.

And Sarah's done something remarkable: She's made it contagious. She leads women's groups at her company.

She brings other women "up the elevator together" rather than climbing the ladder alone. She's teaching joy through action.

"I like the analogy of taking an elevator because, in the elevator, you can bring other people, especially women, along with you," Sarah says. "Everyone's getting off and on at different floors. Mine might stop here; theirs might continue. But I like the idea of going up together because it's a lot more fun on the way up and a lot less lonely if you happen to be going down."

The Vision and Goals Method™ gave Sarah boundaries. It gave her clarity. But more than that, it gave her a practice she could return to, again and again, for the rest of her life.

"What brings me joy?" Sarah closes. "Good books. Vacations. My family. My boys are the sunrise and the sunset. My partner and spouse. We've been married twelve years, and not every day is easy or fun. But that's been a big part of my joy for twelve years."

Sarah knows her joy. And she practices it. Intentionally. Repeatedly. Across all four key areas of her life. Not because she has it figured out. But because she's committed to the practice of figuring it out, over and over again, as life evolves.

Now, as you turn the last few pages of this book, I hope this motivates you to make joy a way of life.

JOY JUMPSTART

Decide on one thing you can do today to move forward in joyful living. Is it a tiny habit to incorporate into your routine? What stood out to you the most as you read this book that's something you're excited to try? Perhaps it's a reminder to show yourself gratitude, support your joy squad, or be in community with others.

This isn't a grandiose occasion, but rather a sustainable shift that you can start today and build up over time.

Notes

INTRODUCTION

1. Matthew Kuan Johnson, "Joy: A Review of the Literature and Suggestions for Future Directions." *The Journal of Positive Psychology*, 15, no. 1 (2020), accessed February 10, 2026, https://doi.org/10.1080/17439760.2019.1685581

2. Maria Roberts and Richard Appiah. "The Complexities of Joy: A Qualitative Study of Joy Cultivation, Loss of Joy, and Happiness in British Adults." *International Journal of Qualitative Studies on Health and Well-Being*, 20, no. 1 (2025), accessed February 10, 2026, https://doi.org/10.1080/17482631.2025.2508946

CHAPTER 1

1. "Broaden and Build Theory of Positive Emotions" in *Psychology of Human Emotion: An Open Access Textbook*, accessed February 5, 2026, https://psu.pb.unizin.

org/psych425/chapter/broden-and-build-theory-of-positive-emotions/

2. Deborah Lovich and Rosie Sargeant, "Enjoying Work Matters More Than You Realize," Boston Consulting Group website, accessed February 9, 2026, https://www.bcg.com/publications/2024/joy-at-work-matters-more-than-you-realize

CHAPTER 8

1. Deborah Lovich and Rosie Sargeant, "Enjoying Work Matters More Than You Realize."

2. "What is Employee Engagement, and How Do You Improve It?" Gallup, accessed February 9, 2026, https://www.gallup.com/workplace/285674/improve-employee-engagement-workplace.aspx

3. Elizabeth A. Kelsey. "Joy in the Workplace: The Mayo Clinic Experience," *American Journal of Lifestyle Medicine*, 17, no. 3 (2021), accessed February 25, 2026. https://doi.org/10.1177/15598276211036886

4. Rozita Jolilianhasanpour, Shadi Asadollahi, and David M. Yousem, "Creating Joy in the Workplace," *European Journal of Radiology*, 145, (2021), accessed February 25, 2026. https://doi.org/10.1016/j.ejrad.2021.110019

CHAPTER 9

1. Michael A. Cohn, Barbara L. Fredrickson, Stephanie L. Brown, Joseph A. Mikels, and Anne M. Conway, "Happiness Unpacked: Positive Emotions Increase Life Satisfaction," *Emotion*, 9, no. 3 (2009), National Institute of Health, accessed February 5, 2026. https://thefpr.org/wp-content/uploads/positive_emotions_fredrickson_2009.pdf

2. Amina Parveen and Suraya Jabeen Qurashi, "Resilience Promoting Happiness: An Attempt to Explore Interdependence," *International Journal for Multidisciplinary Research*, 6, no. 6 (2024), accessed February 10, 2026, https://doi.org/10.36948/ijfmr.2024.v06i06.30819

CHAPTER 10

1. Michael A. Cohn et al., "Happiness unpacked."

2. Toi Derricotte, "The Telly Cycle," in *The Undertaker's Daughter* (Pittsburgh: University of Pittsburgh Press, 2011), 51–63.

Cheers to Your Joy—Past, Present, and Future

You owe yourself a round of applause...

- A round of applause for considering your joy worth the price of this book.

- A round of applause for carving out time for yourself by reading this book.

- A round of applause for making space to identify your joy.

- A round of applause for any action (small or large) that you took to amplify your joy.

- A round of applause for setting boundaries to protect your joy.

- A round of applause for shifting your mindset to understand you deserve joy right now.

- A round of applause for sharing your joy factors with others.

- A round of applause for supporting someone else's joy journey.

- A round of applause for telling someone else about this book, encouraging them to choose their joy.

- A round of applause for any and everything you've done to leverage joy as your foundation for living.

You did all of that. You didn't have to, but you will be more fulfilled now that you have named, chosen, and are protecting your joy as a regular practice.

And now...

- I hope this book unlocked an insatiable thirst for your inner joy.

- I hope this book helped you create a love letter to yourself.

- I hope this book helped you build a strategic road-map for your life.

- I hope this book helped you see yourself in new ways.

- I hope this book brought you smiles, laughter, and even tears.

- I hope this book brought you what you needed, when you needed it.

I am grateful to be on this joy journey with you, so feel free to:

- Tag me in a "My joy is ______________!" post on social media.

- Cheer for others. Celebrate your wins. Connect with community in my #FinishlineFriday posts.

- Email me with how you're letting joy lead.

I wrote this book because joy can be leveraged as both your offense and your defense. As your offense, it's the way you lead your life and make difficult decisions. As your defense, it's how you set boundaries that protect your goals and aspirations. I have seen the rewards of leveraging joy and have researched how leading with joy affects your work, which is why I am on a mission to build the business case for joy.

A Continuation in Joy

Joy is the one thing that can't be taken away from you. It took time, practice, and patient repetition for me to learn how to leverage joy in a way that let me reclaim it when someone tried to steal it. I don't believe I'll ever fully complete this practice; instead, I look forward to continued fine-tuning as I grow. I hope this book helps you do the same in all areas of life. There will be times when joy feels impossible, but I pray you make your way back to your joy, and please know that I'm rooting for you always!

There are times when it's harder to choose joy, and that's when you can come to this book or go to my social media pages for a reminder that you deserve joy as well as a reminder on how to start, sustain, or spread your joy depending on where you're at that day.

Moving beyond permission, you now have language to associate with what it looks like to lead with joy. Keep in mind that progress beats perfection any day. Consider if you implemented one new habit a month, you would have twelve new habits you intentionally added to your life at the end of the year. However, if you tried to implement twelve new habits at the same time, you'd burn out within a month or two. Rather than trying to do everything at once, give yourself time to digest if something resonates with you for at least a month before you add more. Even if you simply do one per year, you are making progress that's sustainable rather than an unrealistic overload. Joy doesn't promise to be obvious or easy, so take your purposeful pauses, making space to see yourself and to remember that this is perfectly normal, if not even expected. You have time—take it.

Move forward from this book armed with the knowledge to practice (not perfect) joyful living throughout your life. Similar to a physical workout, you do it throughout life as maintenance. Think of joyful living as part of your mental maintenance of choosing self, falling more in love with yourself, and fostering healthy communities around you. Joy is your compass in building this life, not just something to aim for in the future. You are now equipped with guidance to choose your joy—use it when fear creeps in, worldly expectations try to take over, or exhaustion is getting the best of your brain power. You know your joy. You are capable of choosing it, so do it.

Let joy lead.

— Rose

Acknowledgements

Goal crushing is a team sport.

I thank my mom for raising a little girl who valued her joy over anything else and for protecting her joy. I love you, my forever joy guardian.

I thank my fur baby in heaven, Chanel, for sixteen-years that spanned our time as Oklahoma girls growing into Chicago women together. You humbled my spirit and prepared me for the journey in joy ahead.

I thank my joy squads in the four key areas of life for the following:

Thank you to my **Personal Joy Squad** for the love, time, ideation sessions, cry sessions, and laugh sessions that got me across the finish line with this book.

Thank you to my **Professional Joy Squad** (aka my Personal Board of Directors) for legal guidance, coaching, experience sharing, navigating this career shift, and reminding me of my value. My clients for going beyond hiring me by getting curious about the book and my entrepreneurial journey.

Thank you to my **Health Joy Squad** for therapy, thought partnership, run clubs, sweaty dates, acupuncture, and massage sessions. You've held my body together (mentally and physically), for which I'm forever grateful.

Thank you to my **Financial Joy Squad** for taking on my least favorite yet most necessary task with grace and grit, and for being patient with me. I can trust you over and over.

**You are all a part of me that makes it possible
for me to do this work.**

You made it possible for me to write this book.

You've helped me spread joy to the world in my business-meets-Barbie fashion, and I love you for that.

You believed in the whole me, NOT just a part of me.

You protected me so I'd have the mental, physical, and emotional space to accomplish this.

You cheered loudly and proudly for my wins.

You empathized with my losses, providing grace, opportunity, and understanding.

You gave me real talk with good, honest feedback at every turn.

You allowed me to hear your wins and be your cheerleader (my favorite activity).

You prayed with and for me, at times unbeknownst to me.

You held my metaphysical hand through life while I worked on the hardest thing I've ever done.

You picked up the phone to check on me, but also answered my calls for help.

You shared client leads and made introductions without hesitation.

You listened without judgment.

And best of all, you laughed oh so loudly at my random dorky quips and attempts at humor.

You are a piece of my puzzle that completes me.

It's a true honor to be in community with you. This book is as much mine as it is yours...I hope you're proud of our work.

I admire you for loving yourself, your joy, and your unique talents.

May you be blessed, moisturized, and hydrated ♡.

I am cheering for your success—past, present, and future.

— Bose

Partner with Bose to Speak at Your Conference or Train Your Team

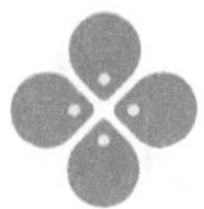

Bose delivers a message of joy and inspiration with action-able steps!

As a professional speaker with keynotes focused on leading with joy in goal set-ting, networking, and team alignment, she has a proven track record of igniting audi-ences. When Bose takes the stage, she delivers a message of hope and success that ignites a spark in each audience member, enabling them to take strategic risks.

Above all, Bose believes that every single person was made for joy. By the end of her message, your audience will believe in themselves, too. Moreover, they will leave empowered, uplifted, and ready to show the world their brilliance within.

Her keynotes are perfect for meeting planners and conference organizers who want to provide their audiences with more than just inspiration. If your goal is to go beyond motivation and into truly practical, impactful talks, Bose is your speaker.

Between her keynotes and training workshops, Bose has a ninety-nine percent success rate, with audience members reporting they would attend another session led by her. With a ninety-five percent actionable rating and a ninety-six percent interactiveness rating, she leaves audiences empowered, talk after talk.

Bose's signature topics include:

- **Vision and Goals:** 5 Steps to Turn Your Dream Life Into Your Real Life

- **Your Elevator Pitch and Beyond:** Building Your Professional Brand and Networking Yourself Into Your Dream Job

- **Purpose-Driven Leadership:** Achieving a Triple Win...a Win for You, Your Team, and Your Organization

If you are a leader ready to let joy lead, partner with Bose to train your team on one or more of the methodologies within this book. She partners with you, as a leader, to understand your goals and develop a practical approach to delivering training workshops within your organization.

Empowering Dreams. Elevating Teams.
Transforming Organizations.

Visit https://www.goalandgrind.com/corporate-training to learn more.

Join Bose's Joy Squad

If you loved this book, you'll really love:

1. My Newsletter

Enjoy monthly tips on joyful living to support your journey in joy. My newsletter shares resources, events, Journeys in Joy, and exclusive content for my email subscribers. BONUS: A few times throughout the month, I'll sprinkle in extra joy jumpstarts via SMS.

Sign up for free at www.goalandgrind.com/newsletter

2. Connecting on Social

Join my community on LinkedIn, YouTube, or Instagram at @goalandgrind

3. Goal and Grind Courses

Continue your journey in joy with self-paced courses designed to support you in all phases of your career from start to finish. Or you can go directly to the area you need support with such as building your personal brand, interview preparation, or salary negotiations. Access them on my company's website at www.goalandgrind.com/courses

Goal crushing is a team sport.

Keep up with all things at www.goalandgrind.com

About the Author

Bose Akadiri is The Joy Amplifier™. She's a motivational keynote speaker, corporate trainer, author, and CEO of Goal and Grind LLC, where she partners with high-achieving professionals and forward-thinking organizations to leverage joy as a strategic advantage for setting goals, building strong teams, and creating meaningful results. *The Stay Joyful Method* is her first book. Renowned for her dynamic corporate workshops, Bose empowers dreams, elevates teams, and transforms organizations.

She is no stranger to major pivots, having moved to Chicago with no job or network and built a distinguished career in corporate social responsibility at Boeing, Salesforce, and JPMorgan Chase.

Bose is a goal-oriented leader who believes in continuous growth for herself and others. Bose is a Chicago Urban League and University of Chicago Booth School of Business IMPACT alumna and a Girls Inc. of Chicago

She Shines Honoree. She was named a Black Woman Changemaker by *The Chicago Defender*, a 40 Under 40 honoree by *okcBiz Magazine*, a 30/30 Next Generation of Leaders by *ionOklahoma Magazine*, and a Leadership Oklahoma City alumna.

Bose previously served on the Oklahoma County Library board as a mayoral appointment and was the youngest member of the commission. She also previously served on the board of the Ladies of Virtue, a nonprofit dedicated to empowering young women to lead with purpose.

As an avid runner, yogi, traveler, and dog mom, Bose believes in finding joy in the four key areas of life: personal, professional, health, and financial.